BEYOND THE CHERRY TREE
STORIES OF THE PRESIDENTS

ANNE E. SCHRAFF

J. WESTON
WALCH
PUBLISHER
PORTLAND, MAINE

User's Guide
to
Walch Reproducible Books

As part of our general effort to provide educational materials which are as practical and economical as possible, we have designated this publication a "reproducible book." The designation means that purchase of the book includes purchase of the right to limited reproduction of all pages on which this symbol appears:

Here is the basic Walch policy: We grant to individual purchasers of this book the right to make sufficient copies of reproducible pages for use by all students of a single teacher. This permission is limited to a single teacher, and does not apply to entire schools or school systems, so institutions purchasing the book should pass the permission on to a single teacher. Copying of the book or its parts for resale is prohibited.

Any questions regarding this policy or requests to purchase further reproduction rights should be addressed to:

Permissions Editor
J. Weston Walch, Publisher
321 Valley Street • P. O. Box 658
Portland, Maine 04104-0658

1   2   3   4   5   6   7   8   9   10

ISBN 0-8251-2807-2

Copyright © 1996
J. Weston Walch, Publisher
P. O. Box 658 • Portland, Maine 04104-0658

Printed in the United States of America

Contents

Reproducible Stories and Activities

Introduction

On the following pages are stories of each of America's presidents. Each story is divided into two parts. The first part is a story about the president's youth. This story will enable students to more easily identify with the person behind the pomp of the presidency. The second part is a biography covering the major events of the president's life and terms of office.

Students will read about a young John Adams neglecting his studies to go hunting, then lamenting that he'd "wasted his youth" as he returns to books. They will read inspiring stories of sickly youths like James Madison and Theodore Roosevelt overcoming their frailties to make great contributions to American life. They will read humorous tales about Jack Kennedy sitting on an anthill searching for blueberries and young Dwight Eisenhower doing battle with a giant goose.

The presidents came from log cabins and mansions. Young Franklin Roosevelt lived like a prince with his own sailboat, while newborn Millard Fillmore was laid in a box used to collect maple sugar sap because his parents couldn't afford a cradle.

Most of the presidents went to college, but Abraham Lincoln had just one year of regular school, Harry Truman couldn't afford college, and Andrew Johnson could barely read and write.

Some of the presidents like—John Kennedy and Ronald Reagan—were witty and charming, but Ben Harrison was called "cold as an iceberg" and Calvin Coolidge waged a lifelong battle against extreme shyness. At nineteen Warren Harding owned a newspaper, and at sixteen Martin Van Buren summed up a case in court. But Andrew Johnson was a bound boy little better than a slave, and Grover Cleveland, at fifteen, was a clerk who had to wash up in a horse trough.

Most of the presidents studied law, but Grant, Taylor, and Eisenhower were soldiers. Reagan was an actor and Carter a peanut farmer. Most presidents came from Virginia, Ohio, and the Northeast, but Carter came from the red clay of Georgia and Bill Clinton from a town named Hope in Arkansas.

The American presidency has been an all-male, all-white, mostly northern European Protestant institution. But the stories point out how many first ladies played vital roles in the White House. Dolley Madison lingered at the White House to save important documents even as British soldiers advanced nearby. Edith Wilson may have been acting president during her husband's illness. Eleanor Roosevelt was the "eyes of the president" as she traveled throughout America during the Depression. Her insights led to many laws to alleviate the suffering of the nation.

As they read the stories, students will learn that all presidents had successes and failures. Some soared to greatness; others watched their presidencies end in disgrace, scandal, and lost dreams. All the presidents struggled and overcame challenges. All tried in their own way to do their duty as President of the United States. They deserve respect for taking on one of the world's most difficult jobs.

Each story is followed by review exercises and activities that students can complete on an individual basis. The Teacher's Guide (page 125) contains discussion questions and group activities suitable for the study of individual presidents. The General Activities section (page *vii*) gives instructions for activities that may be adapted for use with any president.

A reproducible outline map of the United States appears on page *ix*. You may wish to have students research the locations of various events in the stories and mark them on the map.

Presidential libraries are a good source of photographs and information relating to the presidents. Names, addresses, and telephone numbers of presidential libraries appear on page *x*.

General Activities

The activities in this section may be adapted for use with any of the stories of the presidents.

Instructions for Group Activities

DEBATES

Prepare a handout explaining Robert's Rules of Order. Tell students they will use the rules as they debate an issue relating to one of the presidents. Divide students into debate teams. Have the teams research the selected debate topic as a homework assignment and work on their arguments during class time. After the debate, encourage students to think of ways the two sides of the issue might be resolved by compromise, and to discuss the insights they have gained.

MOCK TRIALS

Have students conduct a mock trial of a president who appears to have done something wrong. Assign students to act as a judge, a jury, a committee for the prosecution, and a committee for the defense. Students should research the background of each accusation carefully before the trial.

TIME LINES

Divide the class into groups and have each group research one aspect of a president's life. One group might research his personal life before he became president, another his military career, another his political career, and another his personal life after leaving the presidency. With all groups using the same scale (e.g., 1 inch = 1 year), have each group prepare a time line, illustrated with either original drawings or with photocopied images from books or magazines. Mount the completed time lines on a bulletin board to present a complete picture of the president's life.

WOMEN IN HISTORY

Organize the class into teams to research famous and influential women who lived during various presidencies. Examples are Jane Addams, Eleanor Roosevelt, Frances Perkins, Jeanette Rankin, Abigail Adams, and Lucretia Mott. Based on their research, have each team select a woman who could have become president. Have the teams report to the class about what sort of a president their selected individual might have been.

MINORITIES IN HISTORY

Organize the class into teams to research individuals from minority groups who were prominent during various presidential administrations. Have each team select an individual who could have been president and report to the class about what sort of president that person might have been. Examples include Harriet Tubman, Frederick Douglass, Dr. Martin Luther King, Jr., and Cesar Chavez.

CULMINATING GROUP ACTIVITY

Have students work in groups to create a time line showing the incumbencies of all the presidents. Make sure all groups use the same scale so that the different segments of the time line can be fitted together. A scale of 1 inch = 1 year will create a time line 18 feet long. Mount the completed time line so that it runs around the walls of the classroom.

INSTRUCTIONS FOR INDIVIDUAL ACTIVITIES

1. Imagine that you want to be president. Research the requirements for becoming president, the steps you would have to take to be nominated, and what you would need to do to win the election. Present your findings on a chart.

2. Choose the three presidents who you think were the least effective leaders. Write why you made these choices.

3. Choose the individual who, in your opinion, was the best president to lead us in the last twenty years. Make a poster of that president that shows his major achievements.

4. There are four faces carved on Mount Rushmore in South Dakota—Washington, Jefferson, Lincoln, and Theodore Roosevelt. You have been chosen to select the fifth face. Find a picture of Mount Rushmore, photocopy it, and add your choice, either by drawing it in or pasting it on a picture.

5. On an outline map of the United States, show some of the important places in a specific president's life. Include birthplace, where president went to school, worked, and died.

6. Write a letter to the current president asking that a certain problem that is important to you be solved.

7. Prepare an outline for an essay on a president of your choice. Use these main heads:

   I. Early life

   II. Contributions during term of office

   III. Overall impact of the presidency

   Under each main head, list three subheads, each containing at least two details.

8. After reading one of the stories of the presidents, write your own list of five questions and give them to a partner to answer.

Name _____ Date _____

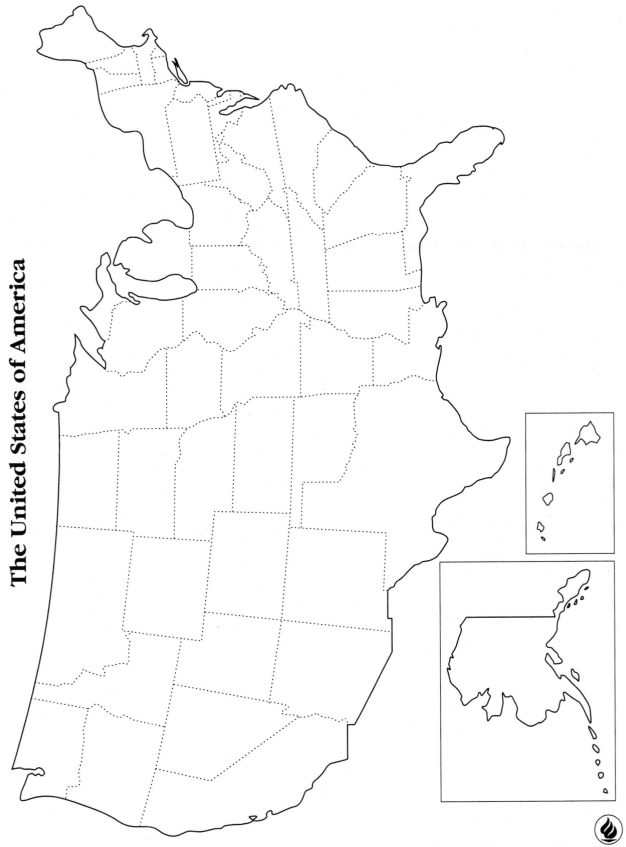

The United States of America

ix *Beyond the Cherry Tree: Stories of the Presidents*

Presidential Libraries

Office of Presidential Libraries
National Archives
Washington, DC 20408
202-501-5700

Herbert Hoover Library
P.O. Box 488
West Branch, IA 52358
319-643-5301

Franklin D. Roosevelt Library
511 Albany Post Road
Hyde Park, NY 12538
914-229-8114

Harry S Truman Library
U.S. Highway 24 and Delaware Street
Independence, MO 64050-1798
816-833-1400

Dwight D. Eisenhower Library
Southeast Fourth Street
Abilene, KS 67410
913-263-4751

John F. Kennedy Library
Columbia Point
Boston, MA 02125
617-929-4500

Lyndon Baines Johnson Library
2313 Red River Street
Austin, TX 78705
512-482-5137

Nixon Presidential Materials Staff
National Archives at College Park
8601 Adelphia Road
College Park, MD 20740-6001
301-713-6950

Richard Nixon Library
18001 Yorba Linda Blvd.
Yorba Linda, CA 92686
714-993-3393

Gerald R. Ford Library
1000 Beal Avenue
Ann Arbor, MI 48109
313-741-2218

Jimmy Carter Library
One Copenhill Avenue
Atlanta, GA 30307
404-331-3942

Ronald Reagan Library
40 Presidential Drive
Simi Valley, CA 93065
805-522-8444

Bush Presidential Materials Project
Suite 300
701 University Drive, East
College Station, TX 77840-1899
409-260-9552

Presidents and Vice Presidents

1. President **George Washington** 1789–1797
   Vice President John Adams 1789–1797
2. President **John Adams** 1797–1801
   Vice President Thomas Jefferson 1797–1801
3. President **Thomas Jefferson** 1801–1809
   Vice President Aaron Burr 1801–1805
   George Clinton 1805–1809
4. President **James Madison** 1809–1817
   Vice President George Clinton 1809–1813
   Elbridge Gerry 1813–1814
5. President **James Monroe** 1817–1825
   Vice President Daniel Tompkins 1817–1825
6. President **John Quincy Adams** 1825–1829
   Vice President John C. Calhoun 1825–1829
7. President **Andrew Jackson** 1829–1837
   Vice President John C. Calhoun 1829–1833
   Martin Van Buren 1833–1837
8. President **Martin Van Buren** 1837–1841
   Vice President Richard M. Johnson 1837–1841
9. President **William H. Harrison** 1841
   Vice President John Tyler 1841
10. President **John Tyler** 1841–1845
    Vice President none
11. President **James K. Polk** 1845–1849
    Vice President George M. Dallas 1845–1849
12. President **Zachary Taylor** 1849–1850
    Vice President Millard Fillmore 1849–1850
13. President **Millard Fillmore** 1850–1853
    Vice President none
14. President **Franklin Pierce** 1853–1857
    Vice President William R. King 1853–1857
15. President **James Buchanan** 1857–1861
    Vice President John C. Breckinridge 1857–1861
16. President **Abraham Lincoln** 1861–1865
    Vice President Hannibal Hamlin 1861–1865
    Andrew Johnson 1865
17. President **Andrew Johnson** 1865–1869
    Vice President none
18. President **Ulysses S. Grant** 1869–1877
    Vice President Schuyler Colfax 1869–1873
    Henry Wilson 1873–1877
19. President **Rutherford B. Hayes** 1877–1881
    Vice President William A. Wheeler 1877–1881
20. President **James A. Garfield** 1881
    Vice President Chester A. Arthur 1881
21. President **Chester A. Arthur** 1881–1885
    Vice President none

22. President **Grover Cleveland** 1885–1889
    Vice President Thomas A. Hendricks 1885–1889
23. President **Benjamin Harrison** 1889–1893
    Vice President Levi P. Morton 1889–1893
24. President **Grover Cleveland** 1893–1897
    Vice President Adlai E. Stevenson 1893–1897
25. President **William McKinley** 1897–1901
    Vice President Garret A. Hobart 1897–1901
    Theodore Roosevelt 1901
26. President **Theodore Roosevelt** 1901–1909
    Vice President Charles Fairbanks 1905–1909
27. President **William H. Taft** 1909–1913
    Vice President James S. Sherman 1909–1913
28. President **Woodrow Wilson** 1913–1921
    Vice President Thomas R. Marshall 1913–1921
29. President **Warren G. Harding** 1921–1923
    Vice President Calvin Coolidge 1921–1923
30. President **Calvin Coolidge** 1923–1929
    Vice President Charles G. Dawes 1925–1929
31. President **Herbert C. Hoover** 1929–1933
    Vice President Charles Curtis 1929–1933
32. President **Franklin D. Roosevelt** 1933–1945
    Vice President John N. Garner 1933–1941
    Henry A. Wallace 1941–1945
    Harry S Truman 1945
33. President **Harry S Truman** 1945–1953
    Vice President Alben W. Barkley 1949–1953
34. President **Dwight D. Eisenhower** 1953–1961
    Vice President Richard M. Nixon 1953–1961
35. President **John F. Kennedy** 1961–1963
    Vice President Lyndon B. Johnson 1961–1963
36. President **Lyndon B. Johnson** 1963–1969
    Vice President Hubert H. Humphrey 1965–1969
37. President **Richard M. Nixon** 1969–1974
    Vice President Spiro T. Agnew 1969–1973
    Gerald R. Ford 1973–1974
38. President **Gerald R. Ford** 1974–1977
    Vice President Nelson A. Rockefeller 1974–1977
39. President **Jimmy Carter** 1977–1981
    Vice President Walter F. Mondale 1977–1981
40. President **Ronald Reagan** 1981–1989
    Vice President George Bush 1981–1989
41. President **George Bush** 1989–1993
    Vice President Dan Quayle 1989–1993
42. President **Bill Clinton** 1993–
    Vice President Al Gore 1993–

GEORGE WASHINGTON

George Washington was not yet a teenager when his father died. George leaned on his twenty-five-year-old half-brother, Lawrence, for support. Lawrence did all the things a father would have done. He taught George how to ride horses and feel at home in the forest.

George learned to read and write and do arithmetic from a private teacher. He didn't spend much time in regular school. As a student he often copied rules of behavior from books, which helped him become a better writer. Following is one of the rules as George wrote it in his exercise book: "Keep your fingers clean and when foul wipe them on a Corner of your Table Napkin."

As a teenager, George had his first big adventure. He spent about thirty days in the Blue Ridge Mountains of Virginia. One night he slept in a rough cabin with only a thin blanket to warm him. Worse yet, the blanket was filled with lice and fleas. Another time George almost burned up when the straw he was sleeping on caught fire. During his adventure, George swam his horse across a river filled with melting snow. He paddled his boat forty miles through rough waters and he shot wild turkeys for food. One day he even came face-to-face with a rattlesnake, but it didn't bite him.

His greatest adventure was meeting a group of Indian warriors. George was thrilled by the sounds of the Native American music they played—the drumming on deerskin-covered pots and the rattle of gourds filled with small pieces of lead. During this mountain adventure young George grew into adulthood in pioneer America.

George Washington was born in 1732 in Virginia. As a young man he was a surveyor. He measured the land so people would know where their properties began and ended.

When war broke out between the British and French, Washington fought bravely for the British. During one battle two horses were shot from under Washington and four bullets ripped into his uniform.

Washington married a young widow, Martha Custis. She had two children and Washington treated them as his own. The young family lived as farmers at Mount Vernon.

When the thirteen American colonies wanted their independence, Washington was chosen to lead their army. He had never led such an army before, but he was brave and hardworking. Everyone knew he would do his best.

The Revolutionary War was long and difficult. General Washington and his army were often cold and hungry. Washington shared the hard life of his troops and they respected him for that. Lady Washington, as his wife was called, joined his camp during the winters. She gave as much help as she could to the ragged and weary soldiers.

As the war went on, Washington learned how to win battles. He used the forest to make surprise attacks on the British. He built fine forts to defend his troops. After many battles, Washington led his army to victory. America became independent.

After the war Washington hoped to return to Mount Vernon and his family. But now his country needed him more than ever. He was asked to be America's first president.

Washington had to set up the new government. He could not look back to see what other presidents had done. He was doing it all for the first time. In a way, Washington had to invent the new government and figure out what the laws really meant. As his wife, Martha Washington also had to become a model for all the presidential families to come.

Washington was not the smartest man in the government. Jefferson said this about him: "He was, indeed, in every sense of the words, a wise, a good, and a great man." Washington spent a lot of time thinking about a problem before he decided. He didn't have Jefferson's quick mind. But Washington always tried to do the right thing. He could have taken a lot of power for himself, but he didn't. When asked what he wanted to be called, he said simply, "Mister President."

Washington led his new country to find its place in the world. That's why he's called the "Father of His Country."

After two terms as president—from 1789 to 1797—Washington returned to Mount Vernon. He could have continued to be president, because he was very popular. But he felt he had done his job. Now it was time for someone else.

Washington said good-bye to the American people. He told them that they should love their country and put the good of the country first. He told them not to get involved in the problems of foreign countries.

Washington died in 1799. As he grew weaker he said softly, ". . . let me go off quietly. I cannot last long."

2   *Beyond the Cherry Tree: Stories of the Presidents*

Name _____ Date _____

Recalling the Facts

Mister   adventure   lived   against   led

In the list below, find the word that fits in each sentence. Write the word in the blank. Exchange papers with a partner to check your answers.

1. In the Blue Ridge Mountains young Washington had a big _____ .

2. In his first war, Washington fought _____ the French.

3. Washington _____ at Mount Vernon.

4. Washington _____ the army in the Revolutionary War.

5. Washington wanted to be called _____ President.

Individual Activities

WASHINGTON IN THE WILDS: DIARY ENTRY

The text describes Washington's trip to the wilds of the Blue Ridge Mountains when he was sixteen. He kept a diary of that trip. Choose one incident from the text and write a paragraph about it as Washington might have written in his diary.

A SOLDIER IN THE REVOLUTION: A SKETCH

Washington's soldiers were often ragged, but in paintings like John Trumbull's *Washington and the Hessians* and William Mercer's *Battle of Princeton,* they are in colorful uniform. Find a picture that shows soldiers in Washington's army. Make a sketch of an individual soldier.

THE BETSY ROSS FLAG AND YOUR FLAG

Washington fought under the Betsy Ross flag. Working with a partner, design your own first American flag. You may use stars and stripes; red, white, and blue; or other colors and symbols. Be prepared to explain why you chose those colors and symbols.

JOHN ADAMS

©1967 by Dover Publications, Inc.

As a boy, John Adams turned against books. He said he didn't like his teacher. Young John claimed that his teacher just didn't pay any attention to the students. But John really wanted to do other things rather than go to school. He didn't mind carrying barley from his father's fields to be malted into beer. But mostly he liked to play. He made model ships to sail in nearby ponds. He made kites and spinning toys called whirligigs. John also enjoyed wrestling, swimming, and skating. But his favorite activity of all was hunting.

John reached the point where he didn't want to do anything but use his rifle. He'd bring his rifle to school and stack it in a corner during class. Then, the minute school was over, John would grab his rifle and go off to shoot crows and squirrels.

One day the teacher found John's rifle and ordered him to never bring it to school again. John couldn't bear to run all the way home to get the gun each day. So he hid it at a friend's house near school.

When John was old enough, he went to the marshes to swim. Afterward, he'd shoot wild birds. Even on the coldest days, he'd lie on the icy ground and wait. When the skies filled with wild ducks, John would begin shooting. Sometimes he skipped school completely so he could hunt all day.

When John turned thirteen, his father reminded him that without education he would have a hard, miserable life. John groaned, "I've wasted my youth!" and finally became a serious student. Books became his constant companions.

John Adams was born in Braintree, Massachusetts, in 1735. As a young man he practiced law. One day several British soldiers were accused of shooting American colonists in the incident that was called the Boston Massacre. The American colonists were really angry at the British soldiers and no lawyer wanted to defend them. But Adams believed that every accused person had the right to be defended. So Adams defended the British soldiers. Many people hated him for doing it. But Adams didn't worry about being hated. All his life he only cared about doing the right thing.

Adams wanted the thirteen American colonies to be independent. He worked for independence in many important jobs. During the Revolution he went to France to get help for the new American nation.

When George Washington became president, John Adams was chosen as America's first vice president. He didn't like this job because there wasn't enough work to do. Then, in 1797, Adams became president himself.

Abigail Adams, the president's wife, was a clever and spirited woman. The Adamses were the first family to live at the White House. Abigail Adams said it was a cold and dark place. She used the visitors' room to hang the family wash to dry. She wrote many interesting letters that leave us a wonderful look at life in early America.

Adams had strong ideas on who should run the government. Men who had good educations and owned land were called gentlemen, while others were called ordinary men. Adams believed only gentlemen were fit to run the government. He did not trust ordinary men to make good decisions.

As president, Adams tried to make America stronger. He started the Navy Department so America would have good ships and well-trained sailors. When he was president, Britain and France were at war.

Some Americans wanted to join the fight. Adams refused, keeping America at peace.

Adams feared that people from other countries were coming to America and spying on America. He thought these people were stirring up trouble among the people. Adams also believed that Americans themselves were complaining too much about the government. He thought this was making the country weaker. Adams wanted a peaceful nation with everyone working together. So he favored some new laws to stop spying and complaining.

Adams's new laws made it easier to throw people from other countries out of the United States. The laws also made it harder to become an American citizen. Finally, the laws punished Americans who complained about the government.

Many Americans were very angry about these new laws. They thought the laws were dangerous to American freedom. Americans had always had the right to complain about the government. This right is in the Bill of Rights. Many Americans turned against John Adams because of these new laws.

Adams served one term as president—from 1797 to 1801. Then he returned to his home. He spent his time writing articles and long letters. Adams died on July 4, 1826, fifty years after the Declaration of Independence was signed.

Recalling the Facts

Circle the correct ending to each of the following sentences. Then exchange papers with a partner to check your answers.

1. Young Adams spent too much time

    (a) hiking　　　　(b) studying　　　　(c) shooting　　　　(d) reading

2. Adams defended soldiers from

    (a) France　　　　(b) Britain　　　　(c) Mexico　　　　(d) Spain

3. To run the government, Adams didn't trust

    (a) gentlemen　　(b) ordinary men　　(c) lawyers　　　　(d) Virginians

4. Adams was worried about

    (a) land fraud　　(b) high taxes　　(c) spying and complaining　　(d) trade problems

5. Adams kept America at peace during the war between Britain and

    (a) the Netherlands　　(b) Mexico　　(c) Canada　　　　(d) France

Individual Activities

ORDINARY PERSON'S PLEA

John Adams believed only gentlemen could run the country. Imagine you are living in 1800. Write a newspaper editorial stating your opinion.

FREEDOM OF SPEECH

Freedom of speech was a big issue in Adams's term. Do one of the following:

(a) Write a paragraph about the importance of free speech.

(b) Make a poster showing a citizen using freedom of speech.

YOUNG RIFLEMAN

Imagine you are young John Adams's teacher finding the rifle stacked in the classroom. Write a note home to his parents suggesting a suitable punishment.

THOMAS JEFFERSON

© 1967 by Dover Publications, Inc.

As a boy, Thomas Jefferson loved to swim and fish with his older sister, Jane. They were very good friends. But life changed when Tom was fourteen. His father died, and he had to become the head of his family. Tom had to help run the family farm in Virginia.

The tall, red-haired boy studied Latin and Greek along with doing his chores. He read many books because he wanted to prepare for college. But what Tom really enjoyed doing was roaming in the forest. It was hard for Tom to sit down on a nice day and read a book. He wanted to climb a hill or canoe down a river instead. So Tom solved this problem by taking a book along when he went hiking or canoeing. Then he could have fun and get his work done at the same time.

When Tom was still a student, he had an experience he never forgot. The freckle-faced boy sat under a full spring moon and listened to a speech. Dozens of Cherokees sat beside Tom. They were listening to the speech too. All had come to hear the great Cherokee chief Ontassete. The chief was telling his people he would soon cross the sea to England. He planned to ask the king of England to help the Cherokee Indians.

As he listened to Ontassete speak, Tom remembered when the chief visited the Jefferson house. Chief Ontassete was a friend of the family. He was also a man who wanted to serve his people. Tom hoped he would someday become such a noble man and serve his own people as Ontassete served his.

Thomas Jefferson was born in 1743 at Shadwell, the family farm in Albemarle County, Virginia. He was the son of explorer Peter Jefferson and Jane Randolph Jefferson. When Jefferson was thirty-three, he became famous as the author of the Declaration of Independence. He was chosen for this important task because he was so fine a writer.

Jefferson had many important jobs, including governor of Virginia. He did jobs for Presidents Washington and Adams. Then, in 1800, he was elected president.

Jefferson made a large land deal with France called the Louisiana Purchase. This doubled the size of the United States. Jefferson bought the land west of the Mississippi River up to Montana and Wyoming. The land that makes up thirteen states, including the Dakotas and Kansas, was bought. This was the most important event in Jefferson's two terms.

Jefferson wanted to know all about the new purchase. So he sent two explorers, Meriwether Lewis and William Clark, to visit the land. Jefferson was delighted to read the reports Lewis and Clark sent back. He especially enjoyed their drawings of the people, plants, and animals.

Jefferson trusted ordinary people to run the government. He was a strong believer in freedom of the press, too. He once said that he would rather have newspapers and no government than a government and no newspapers.

Jefferson was interested in many different things. There was never a president who did so many things well. Jefferson visited Europe and looked at beautiful buildings. Then he came home to design buildings like them in America. Jefferson enjoyed French cooking, trying many dishes. He introduced macaroni and olives into American cooking. Jefferson was also a fine musician who played the violin.

Jefferson was an inventor. He designed a plow, a swivel chair, and a clock that told the time and the day of the week. He invented a machine that wrote a letter and made a copy at the same time. Jefferson kept records of everything he saw on his many travels. He collected fossils—the remains of plants and animals. Jefferson could read in French, Greek, Italian, Latin, and Spanish. Some people think he was the smartest person who ever was president.

The French and British were still at war when Jefferson was president, but he kept America at peace. He once said how proud he was that no American blood was spilled at war while he was president.

Jefferson served two terms as president, from 1801 to 1809. After leaving the White House, he returned to Virginia. There he founded the University of Virginia. Jefferson convinced the Virginia legislature to build the university; then he designed the buildings. He chose the first professors and the subjects that would be taught. Jefferson was very proud of starting that school.

In retirement, Jefferson rode horseback, wrote letters, and enjoyed his grandchildren. Jefferson died on July 4, 1826, on the same day that John Adams died.

Recalling the Facts

Circle the correct ending to each of the following sentences. Then exchange papers with a partner to check your answers.

1. Thomas Jefferson lost his father when he was

   (a) fourteen   (b) eighteen   (c) twenty-one   (d) seventeen

2. As a student, Jefferson heard a great speech by

   (a) John Adams   (b) Washington   (c) Patrick Henry   (d) Ontassete

3. Jefferson wrote the

   (a) Constitution   (b) Declaration of Independence   (c) Bill of Rights   (d) Almanac

4. Lewis and Clark were two

   (a) explorers   (b) judges   (c) senators   (d) soldiers in the French army

5. Jefferson was a strong believer in

   (a) big armies   (b) rich people   (c) luck   (d) the press

Individual Activities

OLD BONES

Jefferson once collected the bones of an American mastodon. What fossil would you most like to find? Imagine you found that fossil, and write a paragraph about it or draw a picture of it.

THE INVENTOR

Jefferson was an inventor. He saw needs and met them. Imagine you could invent something to solve a real problem. What would you invent? Describe it, or draw a picture of it with labels telling what it does.

THE ARCHITECT

Jefferson designed many beautiful buildings. Do one of the following:

(a) Find a picture of a building Jefferson designed and photocopy it. Briefly write your comments about what you think of the building.

(b) Find a picture of any building you like and explain why you think this building is impressive or useful.

JAMES MADISON

Sickly, pale young James Madison stumbled and fell to the floor. His brothers shouted, "Jemmy fell again!" James's mother came running. She always did when James grew stiff, fell, and then seemed confused—as if he didn't know where he was. The doctors called the problem "falling sickness" and blamed it on the boy's nerves. We believe today that it may have been a form of epilepsy.

James always tried to do his chores, helping his father move furniture and doing whatever else was needed. He was the oldest in a family of twelve children. But it seemed he was always sick with one thing or another. Sometimes James had bilious spells that made his stomach hurt. Often he had bad colds.

When James felt well, he played in the woods with his brothers and sisters. He tried to be like them, full of vigor. He played hide-and-seek in the walnut grove. He watched the tulip trees bloom and the redbud trees turn pink in the spring. Then James could forget all about his many sick spells.

But, for James, it was even more fun to go into his father's library. James's father owned many books, which were stacked on the shelves. James took them down, one by one, and read them all. He read thick books about government and science. He loved to read.

As a student, James learned to read in French, Latin, and Greek. He also studied algebra and geometry. Curled up in a chair in his family's brick house, James would read from morning to night until he knew about many things.

Born in 1751 in Port Conway, Virginia, James Madison belonged to a family that had lived in America for about 100 years already. As an adult, Madison weighed just 100 pounds and stood 5 feet 6 inches tall—but he played a giant role in starting the United States. Madison called the United States Constitution the "work of many heads and many hands," but Madison wrote the largest part of it. That's why he is called the "Father of the Constitution." When he was thirty-six years old, he led the Constitutional Convention of 1787. After writing the Constitution, Madison worked hard to make sure it became law. And it did.

Madison set up our special kind of government. The federal government takes care of national business—like defense and dealing with other nations. Each state takes care of things like police, fire protection, and schools. The states and cities fix the streets when they have holes in them. The federal government makes sure we have a strong army, navy, and air force.

Madison was also the chief writer of the Bill of Rights. These are ten amendments added to the Constitution. The Bill of Rights insures such things as freedom of speech, freedom of religion, and freedom of the press.

When Madison was forty-three, he married a twenty-six-year-old widow, blue-eyed Dolley Payne Todd. Her ability to remember names and faces and her charm helped her quiet husband at social events.

With the help of Thomas Jefferson, Madison became president in 1809. Immediately, Madison had problems with Britain. Britain and France were at war, and sometimes Britain stopped American ships on the ocean. Some ships were stolen, and sometimes American sailors were captured and forced to join the British Navy. Americans were very angry about this. They demanded war.

In 1812, America went to war against Britain in what came to be called the War of 1812. It was hard for the new nation to fight a war. The American Navy won important sea battles, but the new American Army was small and lost many battles.

The British Army marched on Washington, D.C. Madison had to hurry away. Dolley Madison remained behind to make sure all the important papers were removed before the British got there. Dolley Madison wanted to save the portrait of George Washington by Gilbert Stuart, but it was taking too long to unscrew the frame from the wall. So she ordered the frame broken and the canvas removed. Dolley Madison barely escaped as the British closed in and burned the White House.

The War of 1812 was called "Mr. Madison's War." It was not popular. People who favored the war wanted the United States to take over Canada, but that didn't happen. Finally the Americans and British ended the war by peace talks. But the most famous battle was fought *two weeks later.* The Battle of New Orleans was an American victory, and it made a hero out of American General Andrew Jackson. Those who fought that battle hadn't yet heard the news that the war was over!

When the war ended, President Madison became popular again. He was elected to a second term. After serving as president from 1809 to 1817, he retired to Montpelier, the Madison plantation. He used his retirement to introduce new ways of farming. James Madison died at his home in 1836.

Recalling the Facts

Using the text for reference, mark the following statements either **True** or **False**. Then exchange papers with a partner to check your answers.

1. James Madison did most of the work on the Constitution. _____

2. "Mr. Madison's War" was always very popular. _____

3. Madison was small as a boy but grew very tall as a man. _____

4. Under the Constitution Madison set up, the federal government takes care of police protection. _____

5. The War of 1812 ended when America took control of parts of Canada. _____

Individual Activities

DOLLEY MADISON'S COURAGE: A MEDAL

The president's wife saved the historic painting of George Washington. Design a medal that might have been given her for her act of courage. Draw your design on a sheet of paper.

UNDERSTANDING EPILEPSY

As a child, James Madison may have had a form of epilepsy. In a current reference book, look up epilepsy. Write a paragraph explaining why this illness should not prevent someone from doing a good job at work.

BILL OF RIGHTS

Read the Bill of Rights. Then list five things you or your family did this year that were protected by the Bill of Rights. Ask your family or friends for help if you want to. Hint: Have you read a newspaper lately?

JAMES MONROE

©1967 by Dover Publications, Inc.

All during James Monroe's boyhood, he knew that war with Britain was coming. When he was a small boy, he saw his father join a group of other angry men complaining about the British Stamp Act of 1765. They didn't like to have to buy British stamps to put on all legal documents and even newspapers. The stamps were taxes that were used to help support the British Army in America.

Young James knew that the American colonists would be fighting for their independence and that he would be a part of it. He was right. While he was still a teenager, James became a soldier in the American Revolution.

James and his fellow troops attacked the Williamsburg home of a British gentleman. They found guns hidden there. The British had planned to use the guns against the Americans, but Monroe gave the guns to General Washington.

Eighteen-year-old Monroe was a lieutenant with Washington in New York. He was one of the few officers chosen to cross the Delaware River with Washington in December 1776.

One dark, stormy night, Lieutenant Monroe was given the job of guarding the crossroad of an important spot. Washington was to come through there later. It was up to Monroe to watch out for the British. In cold, stormy conditions, young Monroe kept his post. Then along came an angry farmer. "You're disturbing my dogs," he shouted, "Move along!"

"I cannot give up my post, sir," Monroe said. The farmer smiled. He brought Monroe food and hot drinks. Then he told Monroe that he was really a doctor and he believed in Washington's cause. During the next few days, this doctor joined Washington's army.

During a battle, a musket ball tore into Monroe's shoulder. It was this doctor who saved his life. Monroe would have bled to death except for the care he got from the doctor he met on that cold, dark night.

America's fifth president, James Monroe, was born in 1758 in Virginia. As a six-foot-tall young soldier with gray-blue eyes, Monroe fought bravely in the American Revolution. He was with Washington at the bitter winter encampment at Valley Forge.

After the war, Monroe became friends with the governor of Virginia, Thomas Jefferson. From then on the two men were close friends. Their friendship changed Monroe's life and continued for almost fifty years, until Jefferson's death. Jefferson taught young Monroe all about the law and guided his path. Jefferson praised Monroe as a very good man, saying he was just about perfect. So Jefferson chose Monroe to do many important jobs for him.

Monroe traveled to France, Spain, and Britain doing jobs for President Washington, and then for Jefferson. He helped Jefferson make the Louisiana Purchase. Jefferson trusted no other man as much as he trusted Monroe. When he sent Monroe on important jobs, he said, "All eyes, all hopes are now fixed on you." Monroe never let his friend down. He always did a good job.

Monroe had served these presidents well. In 1817, he became president himself. His term was called the time of "good feelings." America was growing, and people were hopeful about the future.

President Monroe's most important policy was called the Monroe Doctrine. Its purpose was to keep European nations from coming over and interfering in Latin America. In 1822 many countries in Latin America had broken away from Spain. They had been colonies of Spain just as the Americans had been colonists of Britain. The American colonists had wanted to be independent, so they had a revolution against Britain. The Latin American nations had revolutions, as well, to be free of Spain. But Spain was talking about taking these countries back again. Spain and other European countries were talking about sending armies into Latin America to set up the kinds of government they wanted. President Monroe decided to stop that. He thought Latin America was no place for European armies.

Monroe told Europe to stay out of the Western Hemisphere, which included North and South America. He warned that there would be trouble if they came. Monroe is remembered mostly for this one policy. For many decades to follow, the United States continued to hold the Monroe Doctrine, telling other nations to stay out of the area.

After two terms as president, from 1817 to 1825, Monroe returned to his farm in Virginia. He was interested in education and politics during his retirement. On July 4, 1831, Monroe died. He was the third of the early presidents to die on the Fourth of July. He was the last of the group of Virginia gentlemen from old families to be president. This group included Washington, Jefferson, Madison, and Monroe.

Recalling the Facts

In the list below, find the word that correctly completes each sentence. Write the word in the blank. Then exchange papers with a partner to check your answers.

hopeful   Washington   good feelings

Jefferson   Monroe Doctrine

1. Young Monroe served in the army under _____.

2. Monroe studied law under _____.

3. Monroe's term was called a time of _____.

4. Europe was told to stay out of the Western Hemisphere by the _____.

5. During Monroe's term, Americans were _____.

Individual Activities

MONROE IN PAINTINGS

Find several portraits of President Monroe in history textbooks. After looking at them, write a paragraph about his appearance as if you were describing someone you had just met on the street.

YOUNG HERO: A NEWSPAPER ARTICLE

Imagine you were a newspaper reporter writing an article about Monroe and the doctor who saved his life. Write a headline and a brief news story. Look at newspaper stories in today's paper for style of writing.

LATIN-AMERICAN INDEPENDENCE

The Monroe Doctrine helped many Latin-American nations keep their independence. Look up the history of one country in Latin America. Find out when and how that country became independent. Draw that nation's flag, or write a paragraph about the person who led that country to independence—as George Washington led the United States. (For example, Simón Bolívar led Venezuela to independence.)

JOHN QUINCY ADAMS

One hot day in June of 1775, young John Quincy Adams climbed the giant rocks to the top of Penn Hill. John stood beside his mother, Abigail Adams. They watched the rising black smoke over the blue bay. The Revolutionary War was on, and they were watching the Battle of Bunker Hill.

Young John's father, John Adams, was working to help start the new nation. John's father made many trips to Europe looking for help from other countries. When John was ten, his father decided it was time for the boy to learn firsthand about the world. So young John went with his father to Europe. Abigail Adams was sad to see her son go off on such a long trip. She said it

felt like having her arm cut off, but she let him go anyway.

John stepped onto a big, dirty ship—the *Boston*—on February 13, 1778. John heard the sailors cursing. He smelled the bad water and the smoking coal. During the journey, a fellow passenger had to have a limb (arm or leg) amputated. For the next six weeks, wild winds tossed the ship. Lightning split the mainmast. Then, at last, John saw the villages of France. John and his father traveled through fields of grain, flocks of sheep, and vineyards. John saw castles and convents, and then Paris.

John spent two years in Europe with his father. Once, when John's mother wrote to say John's father was not writing often enough, John wrote this to his mother: "He (father) cannot write but very little because he has so many other things to think of."

John Quincy Adams was born in 1767 in Braintree, Massachusetts. He was the son of America's second president, John Adams. John Quincy saw things that few boys his age ever saw because of his important family. He attended Harvard University, and at twenty-eight, he began doing important jobs for the government. He helped write the peace treaty that ended the War of 1812. He also played a big part in writing the Monroe Doctrine.

In 1825 Adams was elected president as his ninety-year-old father, John Adams, looked on with pride. Adams was the only son of a president who also became president.

Adams believed in a strong national government. He wanted to build many roads and canals so Americans could move west. He wanted to see farms filling up all the empty land out west. Louisa Catherine Adams, his wife, had a scientific mind. She raised silkworms and wound silk from the cocoons.

Adams served as president from 1825 to 1829. He was not chosen for a second term. But he still wanted to serve the people, so he was elected to the House of Representatives from Quincy, Massachusetts. Adams did not mind having once been president and now being just one of many congressmen. He wanted to be useful to the people of Massachusetts.

Adams argued well for the causes he believed in. He wanted to see slavery ended. So he made many strong speeches against slavery. Adams's speeches were so great that he was nicknamed "Old Man Eloquent."

Adams often took unpopular stands if he believed they were right. He didn't care if people liked him or not. Adams was guided by what his father told him when he was a boy. John Adams had told his son that elected people were the servants of God; they always had to do the right thing.

When people told Adams to stop taking unpopular stands, he paid no attention to them. He said he wasn't sorry for standing up for his causes. "I would do it all over again," he said with pride.

Adams helped set up the Smithsonian Institution in Washington, D.C. It has museums and a famous zoo with animals, birds, and reptiles. Many historical objects are there, including the original Star-Spangled Banner, the first plane flown by the Wright Brothers, and Charles Lindbergh's plane, the *Spirit of St. Louis.*

When John Quincy Adams was eighty years old, he stood up and made a speech about the American war with Mexico. Most people were in favor of that war, but Adams thought it was wrong. While making this speech in 1848, Adams fainted. Two days later, he died.

Congressman Adams had done what President Adams could not do—he won the hearts of his people. For eighteen years he served in the House of Representatives. Everybody began to respect his courage and his good ideas. No job had ever given Adams so much joy as being a congressman.

Recalling the Facts

Write either **True** or **False** after each of the following statements. Exchange papers with a partner to check your answers.

1. Young John Quincy Adams watched the Battle of Bunker Hill.   _____

2. Adams was the only son of a president who was later elected president himself.   _____

3. When Adams left the White House, he became a congressman.   _____

4. Adams opposed the Smithsonian Institution.   _____

5. Adams was nicknamed "Old Man Eloquent."   _____

Individual Activities

LETTER FROM SEA

Imagine you are young John Quincy Adams. You have just arrived in France. Write a letter to your mother describing your journey on the *Boston*.

SAILING SHIPS

Look in a large encyclopedia or book on ships. Find the kinds of sailing ships used when Adams sailed on the *Boston*. Select one, and in one paragraph describe the ship's size, speed, etc. Or draw a picture of the ship, using pen and ink or watercolors.

LETTER TO THE EDITOR

Imagine you are a resident of Quincy, Massachusetts, in Adams's time. Adams has been criticized for his speeches and you want to defend him. Write why you believe Adams is a fine congressman.

ANDREW JACKSON

© 1967 by Dover Publications, Inc.

Tall, red-haired Andy Jackson was four-teen years old and, he thought, old enough to fight in the Revolution. But he was too young to be a soldier. Instead, he helped his mother and the neighbors nurse wounded American soldiers in a nearby church. When Andy saw the badly hurt men, he wanted to join the army more than ever and do his part.

Finally Andy begged his mother to let him join the Waxhaws Militia. Because he could shoot and ride well, his mother agreed to let him go. Andy rode off to Waxhaws, South Carolina. He was taken into the militia, but he wasn't allowed to

fight. He was given the job of carrying messages and doing guard duty.

While hiding in a frontier cabin after a battle, Andy was captured by the British. A British officer demanded the boy get down on his knees and polish the officer's boots. Andy hotly refused. The officer grew so angry that he struck at Andy with his sword. Andy raised his arm to protect himself, but the sword blade cut deeply into his hand and head. The scar of the head wound remained with Andrew Jackson all his life. He always felt deep anger against the British.

Andy was held prisoner in Camden Jail. Many of the other prisoners of war were sick, and Andy's mother came to nurse them. Soon she was able to take her son home, but shortly afterward, she died. Andy's father had died before he was born. Now, at fourteen, he was on his own without either parent.

Andrew Jackson was born in the Waxhaws district of South Carolina in 1767. Mostly on his own as a boy, he grew to be a tall, thin, fiery-eyed young man. At twenty-one he became a lawyer, and then ran for office. He was known as a rough-and-tumble frontiersman who often got into fights. He fought two duels. He was nick-named "Old Hickory" because he was as tough and strong as hickory wood.

At the age of twenty-four, Jackson married Rachel Donelson Robards, a woman who had been married before. Jackson believed she was divorced, but there had been a mix-up in the divorce papers. She was still legally married to her first husband. Gossips learned about this and attacked Rachel Jackson, hurting her and her husband very much. Rachel Jackson was a pioneer woman who smoked a clay pipe and wore sunbonnets. She never fit in with gentlemen and ladies from wealthy American families; she always felt out of place.

During the War of 1812, Jackson became a war hero. In January 1815, 5000 British soldiers attacked New Orleans. (The war was already over, but news traveled so slowly in those days that the armies didn't know.) Jackson's men were joined by many black Americans, and even a famous pirate, Jean Lafitte. Jackson won a big victory and became an American hero because of it.

In 1828 Andrew Jackson was elected president, but his wife feared social life in Washington. She died before Jackson took office. He always blamed the gossip against her for breaking her heart and killing her.

When Jackson became president, he invited everyone to watch the swearing-in. There was a wild party with people running all over the White House. Jackson's enemies said this proved he had no dignity and was unfit to be president.

As president, Jackson disliked the large Bank of the United States. He believed this bank would not give loans to small farmers. So Jackson decided to try to break the Bank of the United States and help many small state banks. The state banks would more often lend money to small farmers. Jackson won against the Bank of the United States, but many thought that the president was now too powerful. They made fun of him in cartoons, crowning him "King Andrew I."

Jackson's Indian policy was very unjust for Native Americans. He removed all the Southeast Indians to lands west of the Mississippi River. Tens of thousands of Choctaws, Cherokees, and others were forced from their homes and farms. The trail west for these people was called the "Trail of Tears." Nearly one fourth of the Cherokee people died of disease or starved on the trip.

The Indians asked the United States Supreme Court to help them. The Supreme Court sided with the Indians. But that did no good. Jackson forced them out anyway. He said the Supreme Court couldn't tell him what to do. So even though the law was on their side, the Indians lost.

Jackson was president for two terms, from 1829 to 1837. Millions of poor white people loved him because he seemed to be one of them. Jackson died in 1845 at his home in Tennessee, the Hermitage. A friend said of him, "His awful will stood alone, and was made the will of all he commanded."

Recalling the Facts

Circle the words that best describe Andrew Jackson. Then exchange papers with a partner to check your answers.

1. red-haired   5. tall

2. shy   6. yellow-haired

3. brave   7. short

4. proud   8. humble

Individual Activities

JACKSON IN PAINTINGS

Look at Thomas Sully's painting of Andrew Jackson or some other famous painting of him. Imagine you are meeting him for the first time. Describe in a letter to a friend what sort of person he seems to be.

WAXHAWS BOY

Write a short one-act play about young Andrew Jackson trying to join the militia. Include in the dialogue what he probably said and what the military officers who thought he was too young probably said.

RACHEL JACKSON

Some people didn't think Rachel Jackson had the qualities to make a good presidential spouse. Find a picture of Rachel Jackson. Copy it in pen and ink or watercolors, or write a short poem describing her good qualities.

MARTIN VAN BUREN

Martin Van Buren was thirteen years old when he went to work in a law office. The yellow-haired boy was given the job of sweeping the floor and cleaning the quill pens. But Martin was so good at his chores that he was given more to do. He was told to do copy work; he even helped carry law papers to court.

Matt, as he was called, didn't have much schooling. He spent his early boyhood helping out at his father's inn. It was exciting there because he had the chance to meet so many interesting travelers. This helped Matt develop good manners with people. Matt always loved the law, and he was thrilled to be around people who practiced law.

One day Matt had gone to court as usual. He was listening to all that went on. The court was filled with people who came to be amused. Watching trials was a big amusement for many people. When they didn't like what happened in court, they attacked the lawyers and the judge.

Suddenly Matt's boss turned to the boy and said, "You heard the case, Matt. You copied what was said. Now you present the case to the jury."

Matt was shocked. He was only sixteen years old. He was small for his age. How could they be trusting him with something so important? But Matt stood on a chair to seem taller, and he presented the case to the jury. Matt helped win the case. His boss gave him a silver half-dollar and told Matt he was well on the way to being a real lawyer.

Martin Van Buren was born in Kinderhook, New York, in 1782. The 5-foot 6-inch-tall young man was called "The Little Magician" because he had a magic when dealing with people. He could easily win them over to his side.

Van Buren became a lawyer at twenty-one and a judge before he was thirty. But, even then, he knew what he really wanted in life. Van Buren wanted to be president of the United States. He called that job "the

Beyond the Cherry Tree: Stories of the Presidents

glittering prize." He looked at every job he took as a stepping-stone toward that one goal—the White House.

Van Buren went quickly up the political ladder. Each job was a little more important than the one before. When he became governor of New York, people called him the "red fox" because he was so clever. Van Buren became vice president under Andrew Jackson, who admired him very much. Then, in 1837, Van Buren got his dream—he became the eighth president of the United States.

Van Buren was the first president born under the American flag. He was born right after the nation started, and he was the first New Yorker to be president.

Van Buren was not a lucky president. Right after he took office, the Panic of 1837 started. This was a time when businesses closed down. Thousands of people lost their jobs. It was America's first depression. People attacked food warehouses to steal enough to eat. For a while, it seemed that a civil war might break out. Van Buren did his best to deal with the problems, but many people blamed him for the hard times.

The problem of slavery also caused trouble for Van Buren. He didn't take a strong stand on slavery. So people who liked slavery, and those who hated it, both disliked Van Buren. Van Buren didn't want slavery to spread into more states. That's why he refused to add Texas to the United States. He feared it would come in as another slave state.

When Van Buren ran for another term, he lost. There was a popular jingle used against him. It went, "Farewell dear Van, you're not the man."

The jingle said what most Americans felt: Van Buren just wasn't a very good president from 1837 to 1841.

In 1848 Van Buren tried to be president again. He ran on a third-party ticket and lost.

Finally Van Buren returned to the big house near Kinderhook. He often went on trips to Europe, where he was honored by famous people because he'd once been president. Van Buren enjoyed these travels very much.

In his will, Van Buren wrote that winning the presidency had not given him the happiness he had thought it would. He wrote that he had been governor and president, but that the happiest years of his life were spent as a farmer in his own hometown.

Recalling the Facts

Fill in the blanks in the paragraph with words from the list below. Then exchange papers with a partner to check your answers.

slavery   man   magician   law   Panic

At the age of thirteen, Van Buren worked in a _____ office. He was nicknamed "the little _____." In the _____ of 1837 people lost their jobs and Van Buren was blamed. He took no strong stand on _____. People who opposed him said, "Farewell dear Van, you're not the _____."

Individual Activities

JINGLES

An anti–Van Buren jingle helped end his presidency. Working with a partner, compose a positive jingle that Van Buren might have used to help him win.

LETTER TO GRANDFATHER

Imagine you are young Van Buren. You are writing to your grandfather about your big day in court at sixteen, when you presented a case to the jury. Describe how you felt. Also tell him what you plan to do with the silver half-dollar.

A FAILED DREAM

Van Buren dreamed all his life of being president. He then found it didn't bring him happiness. Why do you think this happened? What is your present big dream, and why do you think it will bring you happiness? Write a paragraph.

WILLIAM HENRY HARRISON

As a baby, William Henry Harrison was rushed away from the family's brick house in Berkeley, Virginia. The British Army was coming because the Revolution was on. It was 1773, and the Harrison family was one of many fleeing. When the British Army arrived at the Harrison home, they stomped into the rooms, dragging out all clothing and furniture. They piled everything in the front yard and burned it. Then the cows and horses were stolen. When little was left of the Harrison home, the soldiers left.

As an older boy, William joined the army himself. The British were not the enemy now, because the Revolution had been won. William would fight the Indians during the many frontier battles of the time.

It was young Will's job to help build flatboats to be floated down the Ohio River. They were long boxes, about twenty feet wide, that carried huge loads of food, gunpowder, and animals. The boats were poled down the Ohio to supply the pioneer settlements. Sometimes Indians hid along the river and attacked the passing boats.

One night Will heard about an Indian attack led by the Shawnee warrior Tecumseh. Will met soldiers who were almost killed in the attack. Will long remembered the name of the warrior Tecumseh. Years later, William Henry Harrison and Tecumseh would meet face to face.

Born in 1773 in Berkeley, Virginia, William Henry Harrison came from an important old American family. His father, Benjamin, had signed the Declaration of Independence. George Washington was a close friend of the family. As a man, Harrison held many important jobs. He was a governor and he started a university. But he was most famous for what he did as a soldier.

White settlers were pushing west. They demanded more and more land from the Shawnee and other tribes who lived by hunting wild animals. Important hunting lands were being turned into farms for white pioneers. The great Shawnee chief Tecumseh said that his people could not

Beyond the Cherry Tree: Stories of the Presidents

give up any more land. He met with Harrison at Vincennes, Indiana, in 1810 and told him this. Harrison told Tecumseh that unless the Shawnee continued to surrender land, there would be war between the Indians and the white people.

Tecumseh and his people would not give up more land, so they fought. In 1811 Harrison led an army against the Shawnee town near Tippecanoe Creek. It was a big victory for Harrison. From then on he was called "Old Tippecanoe" and he was a famous war hero. The Shawnee had to give up their land—and their way of life—to the white people.

Harrison became more famous still in the War of 1812. Tecumseh believed that the Shawnee's only hope was to side with the British in that war. At the Battle of the Thames in Canada, Harrison won another victory. Tecumseh died in that battle. It was also the end of his hopes of saving some land for his people.

Harrison became a senator then, but everybody remembered him as a war hero. In 1840, he was sixty-seven years old when he ran for president. All his campaign posters showed him as a colorful old soldier who liked ordinary people. As he ran for president, his friends gave away little log cabins to remind everyone that Harrison had once lived in a log cabin. (He had built a log cabin for his bride when they were first married.) Now Harrison lived in a large, beautiful house. But people liked to think of Harrison as a simple man with humble tastes.

Harrison ran with John Tyler as his vice president, so the jingle was "Tippecanoe and Tyler too." Because many Americans had no jobs and were hungry, they wanted a new president. Harrison seemed just right; he was elected by a large number of votes.

It was a very cold day in March 1841 when Harrison became president. He spoke for an hour and forty minutes in the bitter wind. Harrison became ill with a cold that quickly got worse. One month later, Harrison died. He had been president for thirty days. He was the first American president to die in office.

Recalling the Facts

Match the numbered descriptions below with the lettered words and phrases. Write the letter of the correct answer in the blank. Exchange papers to check answers.

1. They burned the Harrison family's possessions.   _____

2. Tecumseh was a warrior in this tribe.   _____

3. This happened at Tippecanoe.   _____

4. Harrison was the first president to do this.   _____

5. A personal friend of the Harrison family.   _____

    (a) victory over Tecumseh   (d) George Washington

    (b) British   (e) die in office

    (c) Shawnee

Individual Activities

FLATBOATS

In his youth, Harrison helped build the flatboats that were used to carry supplies to pioneer settlements along the Ohio River.

Look in an encyclopedia or book on various kinds of boats for a picture of a flatboat. Write a paragraph describing flatboats, including how fast they went and what kinds of devices were used to move them. Or draw a picture of a flatboat.

THE UNIVERSITY

Before Harrison became famous as a soldier, he founded Indiana's first public library. He also worked hard on Vincennes University. Draw a monument to Harrison that says nothing about his soldiering career. Use a picture of a university and a library or symbols of books and learning, like caps and gowns.

TECUMSEH

Look up Tecumseh. Read about him and find some pictures of him. Write a speech that he might have given to Harrison asking that Shawnee hunting lands be preserved. Or make a sketch of Tecumseh and list facts about his life.

©1967 by Dover Publications, Inc.

Young John Tyler was a student at a school run by a Scotsman named Mr. McMurdo. William McMurdo was a wise man but a very tough teacher. He thought that boys learned best when they were whipped often. So Mr. McMurdo went into the nearby swamp and cut a good supply of birch switches. He wanted them handy so he could whip his students when he thought they needed it.

John Tyler thought Mr. McMurdo was a cruel man who had no business whipping students. John thought Mr. McMurdo needed to be taught a lesson himself. So John got a group of fellow students together, and they hatched a plan against

Mr. McMurdo. As he came into the classroom one day, the boys jumped him. They pushed him to the floor and tied him up. Then they shoved him into the classroom closet, locked the door, and ran away. As John and his companions escaped, Mr. McMurdo was loudly shouting from the closet.

Finally a passing traveler heard Mr. McMurdo's shouts for help and freed him. Mr. McMurdo went straight to John's house and pounded on the door. John's father, Judge Tyler, came to the door. He was John's only parent; John's mother had died.

Judge Tyler listened to what Mr. McMurdo had to say. Then Judge Tyler spoke the words "Sic semper tyrannis," or "Thus ever to tyrants." This is the state motto of Virginia where the Tylers lived. It means, "all tyrants are brought down in the end." Like his son, Judge Tyler believed that Mr. McMurdo was a cruel man and deserved his punishment.

John Tyler was born to an old southern family on a Virginia farm in 1790. When his mother looked at her baby, she admired his silky brown hair and blue eyes. She said, "This child will be president of the United States."

John Tyler held many political offices before he became vice president under Harrison. When Harrison died, Tyler became the first person ever to succeed a president who died in office. He had to decide what to do. Should he take over as if he had been elected president? Or should he just try to carry on as Harrison would have if he had lived?

Some people refused to accept Tyler as a real president. They called him "His Accidency." But Tyler firmly took over at the White House. Soon everyone respected him as the real president. From then on, other vice presidents who succeeded a dead president knew exactly what to do. Tyler had been the model.

Tyler had strong ideas on many things. He believed only gentlemen should vote. He thought the states should run most of their own business and the federal government should stay out of their way.

Tyler did not like slavery, but he owned many slaves. At his farm, called Sherwood Forest, he treated his slaves well; he thought they were happy and contented. Tyler didn't want to end slavery quickly. Instead, he believed it should be slowly phased out over many years.

Tyler wanted to be remembered for some great deed as president. So he tried to add Texas to the United States. Texas had already broken from Mexico. But many Americans didn't want Texas in the union,

because they feared it would be another slave state. So Texas did not join the Union until after Tyler left office.

After serving from 1841 to 1845, Tyler returned to Sherwood Forest. At this time, Americans were fighting bitterly over the issue of slavery. When eventually the southern states decided to secede from the Union, Tyler was very sad. He didn't want to see the United States break up, but he believed states did have the right to secede. His heart was with Virginia, so when Virginia seceded from the Union and joined the Confederacy, so did Tyler. He felt more like a southern man than an American.

Tyler held office in the Confederacy. He was seventy years old and he owed a lot of money. He was sick and weary and heartbroken. Once he was president of the United States, but now many Americans called him a traitor.

Tyler died in 1862, a broken man. When the Union Army came to Sherwood Forest, Tyler's slaves did what slaves all over the South did when they were freed. They rushed forward to celebrate their new freedom.

Name _____ Date _____

Recalling the Facts

Fill in the blanks in the sentences with the correct terms from the following list. Exchange papers with a partner to check your answers.

Sherwood Forest   Texas   teacher   traitor   federal

1. As a boy, Tyler led a revolt against his _____ .

2. Tyler believed state government was more important than _____ government.

3. Tyler didn't succeed in adding _____ to the United States.

4. Tyler's home was called _____ .

5. Some Americans called Tyler a _____ .

Individual Activities

MR. MCMURDO

Imagine you are Mr. McMurdo, John Tyler's teacher. Write a letter to the principal of the school explaining why John Tyler should be expelled.

A SLAVE'S VIEW

Pretend you are a slave freed from Sherwood Forest. You meet Tyler's widow. She asks you why you were not happy at Sherwood Forest. Write your response to her in one paragraph.

SHERWOOD FOREST

Tyler named his home Sherwood Forest. This was the legendary home in England of Robin Hood and his band of merry men. Why do you think Tyler named his home Sherwood Forest? Look in an encyclopedia and read about the natural setting of Tyler's Sherwood Forest—on the James River, right below Richmond, Virginia. Write a paragraph describing the land and natural vegetation of Tyler's Sherwood Forest. Do you think it was like the lovely green woods where Robin Hood lived in England?

JAMES K. POLK

Nobody could figure out what was wrong with weak, sickly young James Polk. He was born on Little Sugar Creek, North Carolina, in a log cabin in 1795. Jim spent most of his time watching the U.S. mail carriers go by on the Great Post Road. He didn't feel like doing much else.

When Jim was older, the family moved to Tennessee, crossing five hundred miles of mountains and rivers. The boy tried to do his share of the work, but he got tired quickly and had terrible stomach pains.

The other Tennessee farm boys made fun of Jim. He couldn't take part in their rough games. Nor could he do his chores around the farm.

When Jim was sixteen and not getting any better, his father had to do something. He took the boy over a hundred miles to Danville, Kentucky. A well-known doctor promised to take a look at Jim Polk.

Dr. McDowell examined Jim and said he needed an operation for gallstones. In those days there was no medicine to stop pain. Jim had to be tied to a wooden table and held down by the doctor's helpers during the operation. All Jim had to dull the pain was a sip of whiskey. It was a painful, dangerous operation.

Jim was very frightened. He thought he might lose so much blood that he'd die. Many people died that way in those days, but Jim lived. He still wasn't strong, but he had no more pain. He knew he'd never be strong enough to be a farmer, so he set out to get some schooling. He knew that was the way to a good future.

James Polk studied law as a young man. He was then elected to the Tennessee House of Representatives. He met and became a close friend of Andrew Jackson. Polk worked hard for the Democratic Party and for Jackson. But still he was not well known by most people. In May 1844, when he was chosen to run for president, he was called a "dark horse." That means someone who has come out of nowhere to suddenly become important. It was a common joke of the time for people to ask "Who is James Polk?"

But Andrew Jackson and other important men knew who Polk was. They helped him get elected president. Polk promised the American people that if they elected him he would make the United States a much larger country. He promised to add Texas to the United States. He promised also to get the Oregon Territory for the United States. Britain claimed this territory, which included areas that eventually became the states of Washington, Oregon, Idaho, and parts of Montana and Wyoming. Polk said he'd make a deal with Britain to gain this territory.

Polk believed that the United States should rule all the land from the Atlantic Ocean to the Pacific Ocean. The American people liked Polk and what he had to say. They believed his promises, so he was elected president. He was the youngest man elected president up to that time. He was forty-nine years old.

Polk kept his promises, but it wasn't easy. He immediately added Texas to the United States. Then the treaty with Britain was signed adding the Oregon Territory to the United States.

Polk then tried to get California, which was owned by Mexico. Polk offered to buy California and New Mexico territory from Mexico for forty million dollars. Mexico felt insulted and refused the deal. Soon fights broke out along the border between the United States and Mexico. Many Americans wanted war with Mexico. That way, they'd have an excuse to just take California and the New Mexico territory as spoils of war. So many people were pleased when Polk and the United States Congress declared war against Mexico in 1846.

The Mexican War lasted a year and a half. There were many battles, and both sides fought bravely. At one point the United States Army went into Mexico as far south as Mexico City. The United States won the war. In the peace treaty, the United States got California and the New Mexico territory, including Arizona and parts of Nevada, Utah, and Colorado.

Polk had kept his promise. The United States was much larger now. But there were new problems too. Should California enter the union as a free state or a slave state? That would be a big problem for future presidents.

Polk was a hardworking president. He was aided by Sarah Childress Polk, his wife, who shared his deep interest in the country and plans for expansion. During his four years in office, from 1845 to 1849, Polk took just thirty-seven days off. He worked from sunrise to midnight every day. He died just three months after he left the White House in 1849. He was worn out at fifty-four. He had given all that he had to the job of president.

Name _____ Date _____

Recalling the Facts

Following is a list of events that occurred during James K. Polk's life. The events are out of order. In the blanks before the sentences, number the events in the correct order. Exchange papers with a partner to check your answers.

(a) _____ The United States gained possession of California.

(b) _____ Polk was operated on for gallstones.

(c) _____ Polk's family moved to Tennessee.

(d) _____ Polk was elected to the Tennessee House of Representatives.

(e) _____ Polk and Congress declared war against Mexico.

Individual Activities

GREATER AMERICA

Find a historical atlas or a history book that shows the annexation of Texas in 1845, the Oregon Territory treaty of 1846, and the Mexican cession of 1848. Trace the outline of the United States, showing these big new chunks of land. Highlight the new areas with a bright felt-tip pen to show how much larger Polk made America.

PRESIDENTIAL WORK SCHEDULE

President Polk worked too hard. Some presidents don't work hard enough. How much time off do you think a president should have? How many days off in a week, a month, a year? Make a chart that gives your idea of a good presidential work schedule.

FROM SEA TO SHINING SEA

Polk and most Americans wanted America to extend from the Atlantic to the Pacific Ocean. Think of at least two good reasons why this would make America stronger. How does it help a country to have ports on two oceans? What did we gain from the new land? Write a paragraph explaining your answer.

ZACHARY TAYLOR

©1967 by Dover Publications, Inc.

Young Zachary Taylor and his eight brothers and sisters lived in the Appalachian Mountains at Beargrass Creek. All the education the children got was from a traveling teacher who stopped at each farm long enough to teach any children there to read, write, and do basic arithmetic. The teacher described Zachary as "quick in learning and patient in study."

Zachary rode horseback on backwoods trails and hunted deer and raccoon. He fished from the banks of the Ohio River. But sometimes fear interrupted the carefree life of Zachary and his relatives and friends. Indian tribes living in the area—the Iroquois, Chippewa, and Ottawa—were being pushed off the lands they'd always

lived on. The Taylors and other pioneer families were now living on lands that had been the hunting grounds of Native Americans. Battles broke out between the white settlers and the Indians. Some of Zachary's friends were killed in one of these battles. It taught Zachary a hard lesson. His forest playground was dangerous.

When he was seventeen, Zachary plunged into the icy waters of the Ohio River. He swam from Kentucky across to Indiana and back to prove his strength. All during his youth, Zachary planned to be a soldier. He never tired of hearing his father tell him about the Revolution and the battles he had taken part in. Zachary looked forward to the day when he would be old enough to enlist in the army.

Zachary Taylor spent his boyhood in the Kentucky wilderness, but he was born in 1784 in Orange County, Virginia. He spent most of his adult life as a soldier. He worked his way up from a recruit to a colonel at the age of forty-seven. He served in the Black Hawk War, a war between the United States and part of the Fox and Sauk (Sac) Indians led by Chief Black Hawk. The war had started when pioneers swept into Black Hawk's village and took it over. Black Hawk fought back but was eventually defeated.

When Taylor was fifty, he became a war hero in the battle against the Seminoles. Now an experienced Indian fighter, he led

1100 soldiers to Lake Okeechobee in Florida. After much hard fighting, the Seminoles were driven back. Some of them escaped into the Everglades, a thick jungle in southern Florida. Taylor was now made a brigadier general for his success against the Seminoles.

Taylor led a war party into Mexico. They started the fighting that resulted in the Mexican War. Taylor was ordered to march to the Rio Grande in early 1846. After some border fighting between the Americans and the Mexicans, Taylor led his men 200 miles into Mexico. Taylor was made a major general—and the second most important soldier in the army. At the Battle of Buena Vista in February 1847, Taylor defeated the Mexican general Santa Anna. It was the final battle of the Mexican War. This caused Taylor to become an even greater war hero and to be known all over the United States.

War heroes make good candidates for president. People like and respect them. So Zachary Taylor was elected president in 1848. He really didn't want to be president, and he didn't have any government experience, but he tried to do his best.

Taylor was a southern man who owned slaves. But he was very much against the South leaving the United States over slavery. He told the southern states that if they tried to secede from the Union, he would stop them with force. He promised to lead the United States Army against them if they attempted to secede.

Taylor was not in good health when he became president. After being president for just one year, he became very sick. He was helping to lay the cornerstone of the Washington Monument on July 4, 1850. The sun was very hot and Taylor grew weak. He'd eaten too much that day and that made matters worse. He went to bed and died five days later, on July 9, 1850. Taylor was the second president of the United States to die in office.

Recalling the Facts

Write **True** or **False** after each of the following statements. Then exchange papers with a partner to check your answers.

1. As a boy, Zachary Taylor lived in the Kentucky wilds.   _____

2. Zachary Taylor never wanted to be a soldier.   _____

3. As a boy, Taylor wanted to be a writer.   _____

4. Taylor warned the South that he would lead an army against them
   if they seceded from the Union.   _____

5. Taylor was president for only one month.   _____

Individual Activities

APPALACHIAN MOUNTAINS

Zachary Taylor lived in the Appalachian Mountains when he was young. With another student, make a rough outline map of the United States; mount it on light wood or heavy cardboard. Using a geography book for guidance, find the Appalachian Mountains; make a pencil outline of them. Then, using clay or a flour-and-salt-dough mixture, make a relief map.

OSCEOLA

Zachary Taylor fought against the Seminole Indians. Look up Osceola, the Seminole chief. Read about his life. He is buried at Fort Moultrie, South Carolina, because he died in prison there. What suitable words would you write on Osceola's gravestone? Describe or draw a suitable monument for this leader.

INDIAN FIGHTER

Imagine you are Zachary Taylor writing a memo about driving the Seminoles back in Florida. Do you feel any regret? If so, include that in your memo.

When Millard Fillmore was born, his family was too poor to buy a crib for him to sleep in. So they put baby Millard in a box they had been using to collect sap for maple sugar.

Until Millard was fourteen years old, he was a pioneer farm boy. He hoed corn, mowed hay, reaped wheat, chopped logs, and cleared the woods for planting crops.

Millard's parents wanted a better life for their five sons. Farming was too hard, and it didn't pay much money. So the Fillmore boys were sent by their parents to learn a different trade. Millard was sent to work for a clothmaker in town. Millard's job was to untangle wool used to make clothes.

The man Millard worked for was cruel. Once he tried to beat Millard. The boy raised an axe and waved it over his head in a threatening way. The man backed off, but Millard was out of a job. Millard walked 100 miles back home.

Soon Millard had another job in town. He went to work at a cloth mill. It was his job to change rolls in the mill machine every two minutes. Millard longed for learning, so he put an open dictionary on a table. Every time he walked past the book, he learned another new word. In this way Millard had set up his own little school in the mill. He was improving his mind as he worked.

Millard dreamed of a good life. He joined a library so he could read more books. Finally he saved up thirty dollars and left the mill to study law. He was on his way.

Born in 1800 in Cayuga County, New York, Millard always dreamed of a better future. When he saw his parents trying to make a living on the poor clay soil of New England, he knew he didn't want that kind of life. One day a judge told young Millard, "The law is the road that leads to honors." From then on, Millard wanted to study law.

Fillmore became a successful lawyer. He married Abigail Powers, a girl who had come up the hard way too. She had begun teaching school at sixteen to help support

© 1967 by Dover Publications, Inc.

her family. After she became Fillmore's wife, he asked her advice on many issues. Both Fillmores loved books, and it was Abigail Fillmore who created the first White House library.

Fillmore was elected to Congress. Then, in 1848, he was chosen to run as vice president under Zachary Taylor. When Taylor died, Fillmore became president. Fillmore was strongly against slavery, and right after becoming president he had to deal with the problem. Northern Americans wanted to end slavery right away. Southern Americans wanted to keep slavery. It looked as if a civil war might break up the United States if the issue were not solved.

President Taylor had hoped each side would give a little on the subject of slavery. Now President Fillmore urged compromise too. He wanted the people who supported slavery to agree not to spread slavery into more states. He wanted those against slavery to agree that slavery could not be ended at once. So Fillmore supported a plan called the Compromise of 1850.

Under the Compromise, California would enter the Union as a free state. All other land won from Mexico had no ban on slavery. Also part of the plan was a tough law that gave slave owners the right to track down runaway slaves and recapture them wherever they went. This angered people who opposed slavery. A slave could escape to a free state, but even there he or she could be hunted down and returned to slavery.

The Compromise of 1850 was not a perfect plan. But it kept war from breaking out between North and South for a little bit longer.

Fillmore wanted trade with Japan. Japan had been closed to Western trade for a long time. To gain trade, Fillmore sent a group of Americans under Commodore Perry to make an agreement with Japan to let some American products in.

Fillmore had served as president from 1850 to 1853, but he was not chosen to run for a second term. He had angered too many people by the Compromise of 1850.

Fillmore returned to his law practice after leaving the White House, but he still wanted to be president. In 1856 he joined another party—the American Party, which was also called the Know-Nothing Party. This party was against people from many different countries moving to the United States. Party members wanted only American-born Protestants to hold government jobs. They especially disliked Irish Catholics who were coming to America in large numbers. Fillmore, running as a candidate for the American Party, won only one state—Maryland. He now left public life for good.

Fillmore spent the rest of his life helping schools and the poor. He died in 1874.

Recalling the Facts

In the list below, find the word that correctly completes each sentence. Write the word in the blank. Then exchange papers with a partner to check your answers.

Irish Catholics   Maryland   lawyer   clothmaker   California

1. At fourteen Fillmore worked for a _____ .

2. Fillmore decided as a young man to become a _____ .

3. Under the Compromise of 1850, the state that would enter the Union as a free state was _____ .

4. The American (Know-Nothing) Party didn't like _____ .

5. In the election of 1856, Fillmore won only _____ .

Individual Activities

FILLMORE VS. EMPLOYER

Working with a partner, write an imaginary dialogue between young Millard Fillmore and his employer at the time of the axe incident. Write down the dialogue that may have been spoken.

AMERICA 1850–1853

In an encyclopedia, find three major U.S. or world events that took place during the years Fillmore was president. Include the publishing of important books. Choose the event you consider most important. Write a paragraph about it.

THE ROAD TO HONORS

A judge told young Fillmore that the law is the road that leads to honors. Look in an encyclopedia; find out how many U.S. presidents have been lawyers. Write a paragraph telling why you think this has happened.

FRANKLIN PIERCE

©1967 by Dover Publications, Inc.

Young Franklin Pierce hated waking up in the morning on that particular day. He was going off to boarding school at Hancock Academy. It would be his first experience living away from home. Up to now Franklin had had a wonderful boyhood in Hillsborough County, New Hampshire. One of eight children, he lived at his parents' inn. There were always interesting people coming and going. Travelers brought news from other places.

Living at the inn was exciting for Franklin. Many soldiers from the War of 1812 came there to eat and drink. Franklin listened to their thrilling stories. He heard how Francis Scott Key wrote "The Star-Spangled Banner" as the British fired on Fort McHenry.

Franklin loved to fish and trap, and he used his rifle well. But now all this was over. He was going to live at a strict school. It seemed his happy boyhood was at an end.

School turned out even worse than Franklin had feared. The rules were tough; boys were punished for the least mischief. So, one Sunday, Franklin ran away from school and headed home.

When Franklin arrived home, everyone in his family was at church. He waited nervously for them to come home. He especially feared his father's anger. But when his father came home, he just told Franklin to get in the carriage. It was raining as the carriage headed for school. Halfway there, Franklin's father ordered the boy out of the carriage. He had to walk the rest of the way to Hancock Academy in the pouring rain. It was a lesson Franklin never forgot.

Franklin Pierce was born in a log cabin in Hillsboro, New Hampshire, in 1804. His father was a frontier farmer who fought in the Revolution and became the governor of New Hampshire. As a young man, Pierce studied law. When he was thirty-three, he became the youngest member of the United States Senate.

When the Mexican War started, Pierce became a soldier. He fought in the Battle of Churubusco and suffered a serious leg wound. After the war, Pierce made some important friends. Soon he was asked to run for president.

Franklin Pierce's wife, Jane Appleton Pierce, did not want her husband to be president. She didn't want to live in Washington. She was so unhappy at the thought of being first lady that her eleven-year-old son said, "I hope Father won't be elected." The boy knew it would break his mother's heart.

But in 1852 Pierce ran for president. He was elected in a big victory. Then a tragic thing happened. Before Pierce took office as president, he was riding on a train with his wife and son. There was an accident, and the president's son, Ben, was killed. Mrs. Pierce was devastated. Ben had been the Pierce's only living child.

Though he was heartbroken, Pierce had a job to do. The forty-eight-year-old president went to the White House and tried to do his best. Mrs. Pierce also struggled bravely to do her duties with the help of friends.

The problem of slavery was now tearing the country apart. The Kansas-Nebraska Bill was passed. This allowed Kansas and Nebraska to decide for themselves if they wanted to permit slavery. Pierce hoped this would please everybody, but it didn't. Nebraska chose to be a free state right away, but terrible trouble came to Kansas. Before the election to decide which way Kansas would go, hundreds of strangers rushed into Kansas to vote illegally. Some were for slavery and some were against. They all planned to vote for their ideas, and they all hoped their side would win.

The election was not honest. When Kansas voted for slavery, the people against slavery said the election wasn't fair. Fighting broke out; Kansas was called "bleeding Kansas." A man named John Brown rushed into the pro-slavery town of Pottawatomie and killed five men. Then 200 more people died in the fighting.

Pierce didn't know what to do. He begged everybody to stop fighting and to be fair, but it did no good.

Pierce bought some land from Mexico, which made New Mexico and Arizona bigger. He also continued trade with Japan. He felt very sad that he couldn't do more for the country, but the slavery problem was just too big.

After serving one term, from 1853 to 1857, Pierce returned home. He spent the rest of his life traveling with his wife. He died in 1869.

Recalling the Facts

Following is a list of events that occurred during Franklin Pierce's life. The events are out of order. In the blanks before the sentences, number the events in the correct order. Exchange papers with a partner to check your answers.

(a) _____ The Kansas-Nebraska Bill was passed.

(b) _____ Pierce became the youngest member of the United States Senate.

(c) _____ Pierce ran away from Hancock Academy.

(d) _____ Pierce bought some land from Mexico.

(e) _____ Pierce's son was killed in a train accident.

Individual Activities

CURRY'S MURAL

Look at John Steuart Curry's mural that shows John Brown as a fiery man. Describe your feelings about Brown based on this painting alone. Would you like him or dislike him? Explain in a paragraph.

THE SADDEST FIRST LADY

Jane Appleton Pierce was called the saddest first lady to live at the White House. In one paragraph, explain why.

DRED SCOTT

Dred Scott was the subject of a famous Supreme Court decision in 1857—the year Franklin Pierce left office. Research the decision and read about Dred Scott. Then do one of the following: Describe (in writing) what the court said about the rights of people whose ancestors were slaves. Or, find a picture of Dred Scott and copy it using pen or watercolors.

JAMES BUCHANAN

© 1967 by Dover Publications, Inc.

Young James Buchanan bent over the counter. He made sure all the spools of thread were there. He wanted to please his stern father, who owned the general store where James worked as a clerk. James made sure every little thing was done right.

The Buchanans and their ten children lived in a two-story brick house in Pennsylvania above the general store. In the store, James dusted each shelf. He neatly stacked the bags of flour and sugar. He checked the nails and the bolts of cloth. He kept track of everything so they wouldn't run out of something people needed. The farmers who came in depended on the store for everything.

James made change for the customers and kept all the records down to the last penny. He knew his father would be unhappy if even a cent were lost. But no matter how hard James tried, his father never praised him. James's father believed that a pat on the back might make his son lazy or careless. So James respected and feared his father, but there was little friendship between father and son.

When James was older his father said, "Go to college and study law and then you will make a lot of money." James took his father's words to heart. He studied hard and became a lawyer. And he did very well.

James Buchanan started life in a log cabin in Mercersburg, Pennsylvania, in 1791. But by the time he was a young man, he was rich. He earned 11,000 dollars a year as a lawyer. That was huge pay in those days. Most men earned much less than 1000 dollars a year.

Buchanan was elected to some government jobs; his future looked brighter than ever. But then he fell in love with a girl named Ann Coleman. She was very beautiful, and Buchanan wanted to marry her, but her. But her parents disliked him. Because of this, Ann Coleman refused to marry Buchanan. Soon after they broke up, she died. Buchanan chose to never marry anyone else. Almost fifty years later, when Buchanan died, among his papers were found a bundle of love letters from Ann Coleman.

Buchanan was sent by President Andrew Jackson on a mission to Russia. Then Buchanan was elected senator. In 1856 he ran for president. He was elected president—the only unmarried man to be elected to that office.

When Buchanan arrived at the White House, the slavery issue was at a boiling point. Feelings ran very high. Two days after Buchanan became president, the Supreme Court ruled that no territory could keep slavery out. This made matters even worse. The people against slavery feared that the terrible institution of slavery would not only go on, but spread.

Buchanan wanted to be a peacemaker between those who were for and those who were against slavery. He told both sides to be patient, that things would work out. But nobody was listening to the president.

In 1857, hard times came to the United States. Many people lost their jobs; this made Buchanan's job even harder. Buchanan didn't know what to do about any of the problems, so he didn't do much of anything.

In 1860 Abraham Lincoln was elected president, but President Buchanan still had more than three months in office. In those days, the president was elected in November but did not take office until March of the following year. During this period, Buchanan was what was called a "lame-duck" president—or a president who will soon be leaving office. Such a president has very little political power.

In February 1861, while Buchanan had one more month to go, South Carolina said they were seceding from the United States. Six more southern states followed. Buchanan could have sent in the army to fight them, but he didn't. "I tried to make peace between North and South, but I failed," he said sadly.

Some say that strong action by Buchanan could have prevented the Civil War. Nobody really knows. But five weeks after Buchanan left the White House, the Civil War began. When Buchanan left the White House, the United States was no longer united.

Buchanan spent the last years of his life at home writing a book about being president. He died in 1868.

Recalling the Facts

In the following list, circle the problems that Buchanan did *not* have in his life.

1. battle injury

2. tragic love affair

3. stern father

4. dishonest friends

5. secession of southern states

Individual Activities

PONY EXPRESS APPLICATION

The pony express was established in 1860 during Buchanan's presidency. The express carried mail from St. Joseph, Missouri, to Sacramento, California. Mail was then taken by steamer to San Francisco. Read about the pony express riders. Then write a letter of application to be one of them. Stress your good qualities, imagining you are a young person of that era.

THE PRESIDENT'S GUESTS

President Buchanan was a humble man—too humble and quiet, some believed. Once when the British Prince of Wales was visiting the White House with a large group of people, Buchanan gave up his own bed and slept on a couch. Write a humorous news item about this, or draw a cartoon showing it.

ANN COLEMAN

Imagine that you are Ann Coleman. You have decided you cannot marry Buchanan against your parents' wishes. Write an entry in your diary explaining how you feel.

or

Imagine you are James Buchanan hearing of Ann Coleman's death. Write an entry in your diary explaining your sorrow.

ABRAHAM LINCOLN

© 1967 by Dover Publications, Inc.

The saddest day in young Abraham Lincoln's life was when his mother died. Abe was ten years old at the time, and he missed his mother deeply. Abe, his sister Sarah, and their father got along as best they could. Then Abe's father met and grew to love another woman. He married her and brought her home to meet his children.

That morning, Abe and Sarah peered nervously from the little cabin on Pigeon Creek in Indiana. They couldn't wait to see their new mother.

"Wagon coming," Sarah said. Sure enough, four horses pulled a wagon into the clearing. Abe's eyes widened as he stared at his father's new wife, Sarah Bush Lincoln. She was a strong looking, big-boned woman. Right away Abe saw the kindness in her face.

"Here's your new Mammy," Abe's father told Abe and his sister. The new Mrs. Lincoln had three children of her own from her first marriage. They jumped from the wagon too. Down came John, Matilda, and a little girl named Sarah, the same name as Abe's sister. This new blended family had five children who needed to get to know each other.

Abe helped unload the wagon. He carried out a feather mattress and feather pillows, then a walnut chest of drawers. Then Sarah Bush Lincoln grabbed Abe and gave him a big hug. That night, Abe slept on that feather mattress instead of the corn husks he was used to. But the real comfort came from knowing that his new mother loved him.

Abraham Lincoln was born in Hardin, Kentucky, in 1809. He was a poor boy with only a year of regular schooling. Lanky, sad-eyed Lincoln became a hired hand on a Mississippi River flatboat at nineteen. Then he became a storekeeper. He served three months in the Black Hawk War, but he didn't see any fighting. When Lincoln came back home, his store failed. He tried some other jobs until, at age twenty-four, he was elected to a government job. When that happened, Lincoln began to study the law. He taught himself by reading law books, and he passed the bar.

For more than twenty years Lincoln made a good living practicing law in Illinois. He was then elected to Congress. But when he opposed the popular Mexican War, he lost his seat in Congress.

In 1854 Lincoln ran for the United States Senate against Democrat Stephen Douglas. Lincoln was against the spread of slavery, but he did not call for an immediate end of slavery.

Lincoln and Douglas took part in many debates. Lincoln won the debates, but he lost the election. During this time, Lincoln said many things that scared people who wanted to keep slavery. For example, he said, "If you don't want to be a slave you should not own slaves." He also said, "Those who deny freedom to other people should not have freedom themselves." It was clear that Lincoln did not like slavery.

In 1860 Lincoln was elected president. The people who held slaves feared he would free their slaves. They decided to act as soon as Lincoln won the election.

Immediately Lincoln had a terrible problem. Eleven southern states had left the Union over slavery. Lincoln either had to let the United States divide into two countries—the antislavery North and the proslavery South—or he had to go to war. Lincoln went to war to save the United States as one nation.

Lincoln directed much of the Civil War himself, because the Union generals were not very good. The southern generals, like Robert E. Lee, were much more skilled.

In 1863 Lincoln issued a statement freeing all slaves in the southern states that had left the United States. In 1864, in the middle of the war, Lincoln was reelected to a second term. The Union armies were close to victory. A lot of the credit went to General Ulysses S. Grant. He was not a great general, but he was stubborn. He kept on fighting until he won.

After a long and bloody war, on April 9, 1865, the southern states gave up. The United States was one nation again, but the wounds of war were very deep. Brothers had fought brothers, and it would take a long time for bitter feelings to heal. Lincoln urged kindness toward the South. He said there must be no hatred or revenge.

Five nights after the war ended, Lincoln was attending a play in Washington. John Wilkes Booth, an angry southern actor, shot Lincoln. Lincoln died the next day, on April 14, 1865. Lincoln was the first American president to be assassinated.

Lincoln, who had promised to heal the nation's wounds and build a just and lasting peace, was dead. It was a sad day for all America. Lincoln was one of America's great presidents.

Recalling the Facts

Mark each of the following statements as either **True** or **False**. Then exchange papers with a partner to check your answers.

1. Lincoln was against the spread of slavery.   _____

2. Lincoln called for the immediate end of slavery.   _____

3. Lincoln went to war to save the unified United States.   _____

4. The Union generals were more skilled than the southern generals.   _____

5. Lincoln was the first president to be assassinated.   _____

Individual Activities

A NEW MOTHER: A STORY

Write a short story based on the incident of Abe meeting his new mother. Include the dialogue that might have been spoken between young Abe and Sarah Bush Lincoln.

GETTYSBURG ADDRESS: A POSTER

Lincoln delivered the Gettysburg Address at the dedication of a national cemetery at the site of a battlefield. The whole address had 268 words. Choose one sentence from the Gettysburg Address and print it on a poster. Then draw an appropriate picture, or photocopy a picture that fits.

ABRAHAM LINCOLN'S SUM BOOK

During his brief time in school, Lincoln had a sum book, as did all schoolchildren. It was like a notebook. In it he wrote:

"Abraham Lincoln is my name
And with my pen I wrote the same
I wrote in both haste and speed
and left it here for fools to read."

Compose a four-line poem about Abraham Lincoln's life. It doesn't have to rhyme, but it can. Include what you think was his greatest accomplishment.

ANDREW JOHNSON

©1967 by Dover Publications, Inc.

Thirteen-year-old Andrew Johnson was learning to be a tailor at J. Selby's large, busy workshop in Raleigh, North Carolina. He had been sent to work for this tailor as a "bound boy." Such boys were not free to leave their jobs. Once they were taken on, they had to remain—no matter how hard the work was.

Young Andy watched the cloth cutter make white marks on the cloth. Rolls of tweeds and silks lay on long tables to be cut into shapes. When the shapes were cut out, they were passed to boys like Andy, who sewed them into clothing.

The boss, James Litchford, liked Andrew. He said he was a boy with no really bad habits. Andy sat cross-legged in the shop, his fingers sore from often being pricked with needles. The thread cut into his fingertips and made them bleed sometimes. But Andy quickly learned how to set a coat sleeve, iron a seam, or make a complete piece of clothing.

It was a boring routine. To make the time go faster, the boss hired men to come in and read the newspaper to the workers. Andy enjoyed hearing the news of the day. He especially liked to hear political speeches.

One day while going home, Andy heard a woman shout "white trash" at him. He was poor, but proud. He and some friends came back and rocked her house back and forth and almost tipped it over. The angry woman called the sheriff. Andy was scared of going to jail; even though he was a bound boy, he left town. Andy's boss put out "wanted" posters for him, but Andy was gone for good. He soon became a tailor in business for himself.

Andrew Johnson was born into a very poor family in Raleigh, North Carolina, in 1808. His father died of overwork and cold after saving two men from drowning. Johnson was just three years old when he lost his father.

Johnson never went to school, and he couldn't read or write. But he enjoyed hearing other men talk about government. He began to see how important government was, because people had such heated arguments about it.

As a young man, Johnson married Eliza McCardle, a Tennessee schoolteacher. Johnson had taught himself to read and spell by this time, but his wife taught him writing and arithmetic.

At twenty-one, Johnson was elected to his first political job. At thirty-four he was a congressman. Johnson was a common man, hardworking with rough ways. Many people liked him because he seemed the same kind of a person most people were.

Johnson became a North Carolina senator. He was not against slavery, but he loved the United States. He didn't want to see it divide into two countries. So Johnson went all over the countryside making fiery speeches against the South seceding from the Union. The southern men who heard his speeches got so angry that some of them threatened to kill Johnson.

President Lincoln heard about those speeches too. He decided he needed a man who loved the country so much. Lincoln chose Johnson to run as his vice president in 1864. Lincoln and Johnson won, but Johnson made a very bad first impression on inauguration day. He was fighting a fever and he drank a lot of whiskey. When he made his speech, everyone could see he had drunk too much. Many people were disgusted with Johnson over this. Five months later, Lincoln was shot and Johnson was president.

Johnson believed in letting the southern states quickly back into the Union. He didn't want to punish them. Johnson wanted the southern states to deal with the newly freed slaves, too. He didn't want the government in Washington to tell the southern states how to treat the freed slaves. This started an angry fight between Johnson and the Congress.

The Republican Congress wanted the military to take over the southern states that had left the Union. Congress feared the southern states would not treat the African Americans fairly. Congress wanted the former slaves to be given full rights as American citizens. Only when the southern states did this should they be allowed back into the United States as regular states.

Congress passed many laws to give the former slaves their rights. But Johnson turned down all these laws. Congress was so angry that they wanted to get rid of Johnson. So they put him on trial for crimes against the United States. This was called *impeachment.*

Johnson's trial was held in the Senate. He was the first president to be tried for impeachment. If Johnson had been found guilty, he would have been put out of the White House. It almost happened. Johnson was saved by just one vote. So he finished his term as president, having served from 1865 to 1869.

After leaving the White House, Johnson returned to his home. He was elected to the Senate in 1874, but he died in 1875.

Recalling the Facts

Following is a list of events that occurred during Andrew Johnson's life. The events are out of order. In the blanks before the sentences, number the events in the correct order. Exchange papers with a partner to check your answers.

(a) _____ Lincoln chose Johnson as his vice-presidential running mate.

(b) _____ Johnson became a congressman.

(c) _____ Johnson worked for a tailor.

(d) _____ Johnson's impeachment trial began.

(e) _____ Johnson became a North Carolina senator.

Individual Activities

IMPEACHMENT TRIAL

Imagine that you are Andrew Johnson. You have just heard that you have been declared "not guilty" at your impeachment trial. Write a diary entry describing how you feel and how you view the future.

AFRICAN AMERICANS IN OFFICE

Right after the Civil War, many African Americans were elected to office for the first time. Find out about one of them and make an election poster for him. Their names included Hiram Revels, Blanche K. Bruce, Robert Elliott, and John Mercer Langston. You'll find articles describing them in books about famous African Americans.

ONE VOTE—ONE MAN

The senator who saved President Johnson from impeachment was Edmond Ross. He knew this act would destroy his own political career and his life. It did. President John F. Kennedy, as a young man, wrote a book called *Profiles in Courage*. He included Senator Edmond Ross in his book. Read about Ross in Kennedy's book (or another book). Then either write an obituary for him, or draw a political cartoon describing what he did. Your cartoon may use stick figures.

ULYSSES S. GRANT

©1967 by Dover Publications, Inc.

As a boy, Ulysses Grant loved horses more than anything else. His father ran a place that tanned animal hides. Ulysses hated the sounds and smells there. He did all kinds of other chores just so he wouldn't have to go near the smelly hides. Even when he was very small, Ulysses crawled around the huge legs of the the work-horses. He never got stomped on. The horses seemed to love the boy as he loved them.

One day Ulysses' father wanted to buy a new horse. He told his son the following:

"Now, first you offer Mr. Ralston twenty dollars for the horse. If he won't take twenty, offer him twenty-two and a half. If he won't take that, offer him twenty-five."

Ulysses nodded. He ran to Mr. Ralston's house. He said, "My father wants to buy your horse. He told me to offer you twenty dollars for the horse. He said if you didn't take it, I was to offer you twenty-two and a half. He said if you still didn't take it, I was to offer you twenty-five."

Mr. Ralston smiled and said, "Give me twenty-five right away and you can have the horse."

Ulysses knew he'd made a terrible mistake. He never should have told Mr. Ralston that his father would go higher in price. Word spread all over town that Ulysses had done something foolish. The other boys in the village made fun of him; they never let him forget it.

Young Ulysses found out early that he was no good at business. But all his life, horses never let him down.

Born in Point Pleasant, Ohio, in 1822, Ulysses Grant went to West Point as a youth. He was an expert horseman and an average student. He liked arithmetic; he hoped to become a teacher someday. He married one of St. Louis's most popular young women, Julia Dent. Her gracious manners helped Grant throughout his life.

Grant fought during the Mexican War, even though he was against the war. Then, after the war, he decided to stay in the army. He was sent to a lonely post out west, which was hard on him and Mrs.

Grant. So Grant quit the army and decided he would look for another job.

Grant became a farmer in Missouri, but all his crops failed. Then he tried selling real estate, but he couldn't make any money. Finally he took a job running a store, but he didn't enjoy it. He wasn't trained to be a teacher, so he couldn't follow that dream either. Just when Grant was wondering what to do next, the Civil War began. A call went out for trained soldiers. Thirty-eight-year-old Grant joined up quickly. He soon became a colonel, and then a brigadier general.

Grant's first important battle was the capture of Fort Donelson in Tennessee. Grant wasn't a great general, but he never gave up. President Lincoln did not have many good generals, so he liked Grant. He said of Grant, "I need this man! He fights!"

Grant led his army to victory at Shiloh, Vicksburg, and other battles. But great numbers of his men were wounded and killed. Some people blamed Grant for being willing to take so many casualties. They said he fought on too long—at too great a cost in the lives of soldiers. But Grant knew just one way to fight—keep on going until he won.

Grant was finally given command of all the Union forces. In 1865, southern General Robert E. Lee surrendered to Grant, ending the Civil War. Grant was made a full general. The only other American to hold that rank was George Washington.

Grant was a very popular war hero. He was easily elected president in 1868. Grant was loved and admired by the people, but he didn't know much about being president. He chose his close friends for top jobs in the government. Grant himself was a very honest man, and he couldn't imagine that his friends weren't honest too. But some were not.

During Grant's two terms in office, from 1869 to 1877, some of his friends stole money from the government. Grant never understood what was going on; he refused to turn against his dishonest friends.

When Grant left office in 1877, he had no money. Later was very ill with cancer. He was worried about his family: What would they live on after he died? So Grant began to write a book about his life. He had had an exciting life, and he hoped the book would sell many copies. Grant finished writing his book in 1885, just four days before his death. The book was the big success Grant hoped for, making $450,000. The family he loved could now live off money from the book.

Grant was an honest, brave man, but he was not suited to be president. He will always be remembered as the soldier who led Union forces to victory and saved the United States during the Civil War.

Name _____   Date _____

Recalling the Facts

Fill in the blanks in the sentences with words from the following list. Then exchange papers with a partner to check your answers.

dishonest   Horses   Mexican War   Fort Donelson   Washington

1. _____ were young Grant's favorite animals.

2. _____ was the only other full general in U.S. history.

3. Many of Grant's friends in government were _____ .

4. Grant's first important battle was at _____ .

5. Even though he opposed it, Grant fought in the _____ .

Individual Activities

PRIVATE LYONS WAKEMAN

Private Lyons Wakeman was a twenty-year-old Union Army soldier who fought under Grant's leadership. This soldier wrote back home about the loneliness and fear in the Civil War. Wakeman died in 1864 in the Louisiana Red River campaign. Wakeman's tombstone reads "4066 Lyons Wakeman N.Y." But this soldier had a secret. The soldier was a woman named Sarah Rosetta Wakeman, one of 400 young women who posed as men so they could fight in the Civil War. Write a suitable obituary for this Civil War soldier, making special mention of the fact that she was a woman.

A GRANT PROFILE

Read about Ulysses S. Grant's childhood, war experiences, and presidency. Then make a chart showing what you consider his good and bad qualities. For example, one good quality surely was persistence.

THE MAN WHO LOVED HORSES

Grant never lost his admiration for horses. At the end of his life, he still loved them. To symbolize this, make a poster of Grant and horses. Or, write a poem— perhaps a limerick—about why he may have preferred horses to many people.

RUTHERFORD B. HAYES

©1967 by Dover Publications, Inc.

Two and a half months before Rutherford B. Hayes was born, his father died. Rutherford was born so weak and sick that a neighbor said, "It would be a mercy if the child would die." But his mother refused to believe that. She called her son Ruddy, and she worked hard to make him strong.

When Ruddy's older brother, Lorenzo, died skating on an icy pond, Ruddy's mother became overprotective of her only remaining son. She made up her mind to protect him from all dangers. She heaped his plates high with food and refused to let him do chores. Ruddy was not even allowed to go to school or play outside for fear some harm would come to him.

Ruddy spent all his time playing indoors with his sister, Fanny, until one day Uncle Sardis came to visit. He demanded to know why Ruddy was being raised in such a strange way. Ruddy's mother said, "My children are perfectly well, but I am filled with fear for them." Uncle Sardis convinced her to give Ruddy a normal life. At last the boy and his sister raced out into the fields.

To make up for lost time, Ruddy made many friends. Some of them teased him about the way he used to live by chanting, "Rud, Rud, look out for mud!" Ruddy became a crack rifle shot (as did Fanny), and he joined the local baseball team. Ruddy helped the farm workers press apples into cider. The boy who'd never done chores was soon painting the house, digging a well, and joining a secret club called the Cobwebs. He excelled at speaking; at sixteen he was called a "first-rate fellow" by his school companions.

Rutherford Hayes was born in 1822 in Delaware, Ohio. His much-loved older sister always told him he would someday be "somebody important." This helped Hayes to believe in himself. He became a good college student and then a lawyer. He held some important government jobs in Ohio.

When the Civil War came, the thirty-nine-year-old lawyer was eager to do his part. He said, "I would prefer to go into the war even if I knew I was to be killed rather than take no part in it." Hayes was in several battles, and he became a hero. When he returned home after the war, he was elected to Congress. Then he became governor of Ohio and was very successful, because he was honest and thrifty. Hayes was admired by all those people who were sick of dishonesty in government.

In 1876 the Republicans wanted Hayes to run for president. The last Republican president, Ulysses S. Grant, had left people feeling bad. There were many dishonest men in Grant's administration. So the Republicans wanted a man who wouldn't put up with dishonesty this time.

Hayes didn't expect to win in 1876. He didn't look forward to the job if he did win, because he thought it was just too big a job for him to do. But when the votes were counted in 1876, Hayes didn't know if he had won or not. The Democrat, Samuel Tilden, won most of the popular votes. But Tilden did not win enough votes in the Electoral College.

In the Electoral College, every state is given as many electoral votes as there are senators and congresspersons in that state. So if a state has two senators (all states do) and six congresspersons, that state has eight electoral votes. Any candidate who gets the most popular votes in that state wins all the electoral votes. To win in the Electoral College and become president, a candidate has to get most of the votes in enough states to add up to a winning number. It is possible for a candidate to get most of the popular vote in many states, but to lose the popular vote in big states with a lot of electoral votes—and therefore to lose the election. It is possible for a candidate to win just the big states, lose everywhere else, and become president.

Since nobody had enough electoral votes to become president in 1876, a group was formed to decide who had really won the election. This group finally decided that Hayes had won. The Democrats felt as if they had been robbed. They pointed out that Tilden, not Hayes, won most of the votes. They began calling Hayes names like "Rutherfraud Hayes" and "his fraudulency." But if the election was stolen from the Democrats, it wasn't Hayes's fault. He took no part in deciding the election.

Hayes did become president, and he turned out to be a stern and moral president. He served from 1877 to 1881 with the help of his wife, Lucy. She refused to serve any liquor at the White House, so she was nicknamed "Lemonade Lucy." Her concern for the people was well known, and she was a beloved woman. At her death, flags were lowered to half-mast in many states.

Hayes pulled the United States Army out of the southern states and gave those states the right to run their own business. But in many of those states, the African Americans were quickly pushed down to the role of second-class citizens. They lost the rights they had gained immediately after the Civil War.

After leaving the white House, Hayes devoted himself to good works until his death in 1893.

Recalling the Facts

Circle the word or words that best complete each of the following sentences. Then exchange papers with a partner to check your answers.

1. Before he was born, Hayes lost his (a) sister (b) father (c) mother (d) best friend

2. Hayes's mother (a) overworked him (b) neglected him (c) overprotected him
   (d) turned on him

3. The 1876 popular vote was won by (a) Tilden (b) Grant (c) Hayes (d) Lincoln

4. At the White House, Mrs. Hayes banned (a) gossip (b) politics at dinner (c) liquor
   (d) business

5. As president, Hayes was (a) warm and witty (b) cold and sad (c) confused by his job
   (d) stern and moral

Individual Activities

RUDDY'S UNCLE: A DIALOGUE

With the help of a partner, write a dialogue between Ruddy's uncle and Ruddy's mother about how Ruddy is being raised. Show Uncle Sardis saying what he might have said to change the mother's mind in the end.

THOMAS EDISON'S LIGHT: LETTER

In 1879, during the presidency of Rutherford B. Hayes, Thomas Edison invented the first practical electric lamp. Imagine your family has just bought its first electric lamp. Write a letter to a friend explaining the improvement over the oil lamps you have been using.

ELECTION POSTER FOR GOVERNOR

Make an election poster for Rutherford B. Hayes when he campaigned for—and won—the governorship of Ohio. Emphasize his war heroism and the honesty that carried him through.

JAMES A. GARFIELD

© 1967 by Dover Publications, Inc.

Husky, handsome, sixteen-year-old James Garfield set out for the waterfront of Cleveland, Ohio. He had been the head of his family ever since he could remember. His father had died when he was two. As soon as James was old enough to hold tools, he had chopped wood and done farm chores. But he had read a lot too. His favorite stories were about the sea, and he promised himself he'd be on a boat one day. He'd leave the dreary farm and have wonderful adventures like the ones he had read about.

"Please don't go, Jim," his mother had begged. She worried about Jim going to the tough Cleveland waterfront on Lake Erie.

But Jim felt like an adult; he was determined to see more of the world.

Now Jim looked around excitedly at all the ships in Cleveland. One boat, the *Evening Star*, was hiring. Jim signed on.

"Remember now," Jim's boss said, "crooks will try to steal the cargo. Stand firm, boy!"

Jim wasn't afraid of using his fists to protect the cargo. But he had one problem. He couldn't swim!

And one dark night he almost died in Lake Erie. The currents changed and the boat began to rock. Jim lost his balance and tumbled into the lake.

"Help!" Jim screamed. "I'm drowning!" But nobody heard him. Jim feared he was about to die. He grabbed for a rope that had fallen over with him. He tightened his fingers on it and slowly dragged himself back on board. Jim had lived through his first sea adventure—even if it was only on Lake Erie!

Jim had to stand his ground against thieves many times. Then he caught malaria and went home to the farm to get well. His career on boats was short-lived—now he would study to be a teacher.

Born in Orange, Ohio, in 1831, James Garfield became a teacher at eighteen. Some of his students were older and bigger than he was. Sometimes they tried to beat him up, but he always got the best of them.

At twenty-six, Garfield was the head of his school; he studied law on the side. Since he had strong anti-slavery ideas, he joined the Republican Party. He married Lucretia Crete Rudolph, a warm, intelligent woman who shared her husband's love of books.

During the Civil War, Garfield joined the Union Army, quickly becoming an officer. He won his first battle at Middle Creek, Kentucky. He fought in the bloody battles of Shiloh and Chickamauga. Then, after the war, the young hero was elected to Congress. He served in Congress for the next seventeen years.

Some of the crooked deals of the Grant administration cast their shadow on Garfield and almost ruined his career. But he told the people of Ohio that he was honest, and they believed him.

In 1880, the Republicans wanted to choose a strong person to run for president. A lot of men wanted the job, and the Republican convention was noisy with fighting and shouting. The Republicans voted thirty-five times, and they still couldn't agree on a candidate. Then they turned to James Garfield. At forty-nine, he was not well known outside Ohio. But he was a war hero and he seemed like a good man. The Republicans voted again, and this time they all agreed on Garfield. He ran for president and won.

When Garfield went to the White House, there were hundreds of men demanding government jobs. It was called the "spoils system," based on the saying "to the victor belongs the spoils." In that time, when an election was held, many people who had been working for the president lost their jobs. The new president then filled those jobs with his supporters. So with victory, the president got the chance to hand out many fine government jobs.

A man named Charles Guiteau was one of the job hunters. As Garfield ran for president, Guiteau wanted to write speeches for him, but he wasn't hired. So Guiteau wrote the speeches anyway. He stood on street corners and made speeches for Garfield. When Garfield was elected, Guiteau was sure it was because of him. Now he wanted to be rewarded with a job.

Guiteau met with President Garfield, but no job was promised. Guiteau wrote many letters to the president. Then he came to visit the White House and became a pest. They wouldn't let him see the president. This made Guiteau very angry. He believed he had helped elect Garfield, and now Garfield had turned his back on him.

On July 2, 1881, Guiteau lay in wait for Garfield. He shot the president twice. For the next eleven weeks Garfield fought blood poisoning. His courageous wife was constantly at his side, and she gained the admiration of the nation. Garfield finally died in September. He had been president for only six months. He never had the chance to show what he could do. It was a sad day for America.

Recalling the Facts

Fill in the blanks in the following paragraph with either the name of Garfield or Guiteau. Then exchange papers with a partner to check your answers.

_____ wanted a job, so he wrote speeches for _____ .

When _____ was elected president, _____ came look-

ing for his reward. On July 2, 1881, _____ shot _____ .

Individual Activities

NEAR DROWNING: A DIARY ENTRY

Garfield kept a diary and often wrote in it. Imagine you are Garfield after the night he almost drowned. Write an entry in the diary telling what happened and how you felt.

PORTRAIT OF GARFIELD: A DESCRIPTION

Find several pictures of Garfield, including some in color. Note the color of his eyes and hair. Was he tall, short, thin, or heavy? Write a description of Garfield, including whether he looked older or younger than he actually was.

THE UNWRITTEN STORY

When a president dies soon after reaching the White House, we all wonder what kind of president he might have been if he had lived. Imagine that Garfield had served a full four-year term. Based on the kind of a man he was, what kind of president do you think he would have made? Write your answer in one paragraph.

CHESTER A. ARTHUR

©1967 by Dover Publications, Inc.

Chester Arthur was called "Chet" by his friends. While he was still a boy, he enjoyed writing plays for a popular magazine. In his plays, the good people always came out on top. The bad people got punished. These are called "morality plays" because they teach a moral.

Chet had a strong streak of mischief in him too. His idea of fun could sometimes be dangerous. Chet and his friends liked to jump on and off slow-moving trains. Once the boys tossed the school bell into the Erie Canal. Chet carved his name on several school buildings when nobody was looking.

While very young, Chet became a teacher. His students were eight years old and up. Once he asked all the students to learn sayings to recite to their parents on parents' night. But one little boy named Asa just couldn't do what Chet asked. Asa told his teacher he couldn't learn the saying. Then Asa expected a birch-rod whipping from his teacher.

Instead, Chet smiled at the trembling boy and asked, "Why can't you learn the saying?"

"It is too hard," the boy said.

"I will find you a saying that is easier. I'll write it down for you," Chet said.

Little Asa still didn't think he could learn a saying. He was sure he couldn't recite it for all those parents. But Chet smiled and said he could do it.

When parents' night came, little Asa did well. He was so proud of himself. And he said he learned the saying because his teacher was so kind and encouraging. So when Asa grew up and became a father, he named his first son Chester Arthur Stillman.

Born in Vermont in 1830, Chester A. Arthur spent his very early years as a teacher. Then he studied law. He became a lawyer and won great praise for one of his cases. Eight African Americans had been arrested as runaway slaves. Arthur proved that they weren't runaway slaves at all, but free-born black Americans. He won their freedom.

Another African-American woman, Lizzie Jennings, came to Arthur for help. She wasn't allowed to ride the streetcar to work because of her color. Arthur won her case too. He forced the streetcar company to make up for the trouble they had caused her by giving her money.

Arthur joined the Republican Party and served in many government jobs. He worked hard for the election of President Grant. For this he was rewarded with a very good job. He became the New York Collector of Customs. In this job, Arthur had control over 1000 jobs, and this gave him great power. Many people tried to make friends with him so they'd get one of these jobs.

At the 1880 Republican convention, James A. Garfield was chosen to run as president, with Arthur as vice president. Arthur was a well-mannered, 6-foot 2-inch man with a lot of charm.

Six months after Arthur took office as vice president, he became president. Garfield had been assassinated. Like everyone else, Arthur felt very sad about the death of the president. Now that he was president himself, he wanted to do something to prevent such a tragedy from happening again. He wanted to end the spoils system, which the man who killed Garfield had been trying to use.

Arthur helped introduce a new way of finding people for government jobs. Anybody who wanted a job would be given a written test for knowledge and skills. Those getting the best grades got the jobs. It would no longer depend on whom you knew. It would depend on *what* you knew.

The Pendleton Act—the merit system law—was the beginning of Civil Service reform in the United States. People were no longer fired when a new president came in. Most government jobs were Civil Service jobs. That meant that if you were doing a good job, you could keep your job when a new president began working.

Just five months before he became vice president, Arthur's wife, Ellen Herndon Arthur, died. She left their ten-year-old daughter, Nellie. Arthur's youngest sister moved into the White House to help with Nellie and the duties of a first lady. Arthur honored the memory of his wife daily by placing a bouquet of fresh flowers in front of her picture.

Arthur enjoyed a lot of people coming to the White House for dinner. There were huge dinners during his term, with many different kinds of food. Arthur was also a sportsman. He was one of the country's best salmon fishers.

Arthur was not eager to be president again. So he served just one term, from 1881 to 1885. He then returned to his law practice. Unfortunately, he lived just another two years, dying at age fifty-six in 1886. Arthur was not expected to be a good president, but he surprised everyone by doing a fine job.

Recalling the Facts

Circle the correct ending to each of the following sentences. Then exchange papers with a partner to check your answers.

1. As a very young man, Arthur was a   (a) doctor   (b) teacher   (c) farmer
   (d) storekeeper

2. The Pendleton Act started the   (a) merit system   (b) spoils system   (c) fishing rules
   (d) trade laws

3. Lizzie Jennings had been refused   (a) a job   (b) service in a store
   (c) a seat on a streetcar   (d) the right to vote

4. Arthur was skilled as a (a) salmon fisher (b) tennis player (c) swimmer (d) horseman

5. Arthur placed daily flowers at a picture of   (a) Garfield   (b) his mother
   (c) Martha Washington   (d) his wife

Individual Activities

MERIT SYSTEM

Imagine that your uncle is a postmaster general. He has always promised you a job when you finish school. Your grades are not very good, so you are glad it will be so easy to get a job. Now the merit system has been established. Write your point of view about this in one paragraph.

PRESIDENT ARTHUR'S LANDAU

President Arthur liked to ride around in a beautiful landau carriage. Find a picture of this or a similar carriage of the 1880's. Then write a newspaper ad, similar to today's automobile ads in the paper. Draw a picture of the landau or other carriage for your ad, or photocopy one.

THE UNPLANNED PRESIDENCY

Chester Arthur was a hardworking man, but he never dreamed of being president. He didn't work toward that goal as many men did. Do you think a person who has no great ambition to be president would be a better president? Answer in one paragraph.

GROVER CLEVELAND

Fat, round-faced "Grove" Cleveland had blue eyes and sandy hair. He could swim and wrestle better than any of the other boys in Fayetteville, New York. One of a family of nine children, Grove knew that money was often short. So he was always looking for a way to make a little extra.

Summers were a favorite time to make money. Grove became a fine fisherman on the shores of Green Lake and along Limestone Creek. Grove loved the Erie Canal too, and he made friends with the men who offered boats for hire. He ran around to find people who had products like limestone to ship on the boats. Every time he

matched a shipment to a boat, he made ten cents.

When Grove was fifteen, he worked for a store owner for fifty dollars a year and room and board. It was hard, boring work, but the family needed money. Grove's father was sick, and there were all those children to feed.

Grove moved heavy boxes from morning to night. He lived in a small, cold room on the second floor. He slept on a bed with a cornhusk mattress. Young Grove washed up in the same place at the curb where the horses drank.

At sixteen, Grove found another job. He taught at a school for the blind. He hated the work, because the blind children were treated harshly. There were tough rules and no fun. It was cold and damp and the food was terrible. It was sad to see such things and not be able to do anything about them. Grove thought that when he was an adult he'd somehow make life better for people.

Born in Caldwell, New Jersey, in 1837, Grover Cleveland studied law. Soon he was working as a government lawyer. He built a fine record for fairness and honesty. Then he was elected sheriff, and finally mayor of Buffalo, New York. As mayor, Cleveland fired corrupt employees and became a hero to honest people.

In 1882, forty-five-year-old Cleveland was elected governor of New York. He was so honest that he was very much feared by dishonest men in both parties. In 1884, stories of crooked deals in government shook the nation. People were sick and tired of crooks stealing their money. So the time seemed right for a man like Grover Cleveland to run for president.

One man said of Cleveland, "We love him most for the enemies he has made." Cleveland made enemies of all those who were dishonest and feared being caught.

The election of 1884 was very dirty. Republican James Blaine ran against Cleveland. Blaine's friends attacked Cleveland every way they could think of. First they said he was bad because he was a Democrat, and the Democrats were the party of "rum, Romanism, and rebellion." That was an attack on Irish Democrats who drank and practiced the Roman Catholic religion. It was also a reminder that the states that seceded from the Union were governed by Democrats. The Blaine people also criticized Cleveland for being in his late forties and not yet married.

The Democrats struck back with this jingle about Blaine: "Blaine, Blaine, the continental liar from the state of Maine."

Cleveland was elected president at the age of forty-eight. A year later he married twenty-one-year-old Frances Folsom. He became the first president to be married in the White House. Five children were born to the Clevelands, and the usually quiet presidential home became a merry place with young children running around.

Cleveland opened thousands of acres of land to small farmers. People who had never owned land before now had farms. When Cleveland ran for reelection, he lost to Benjamin Harrison. But then, four years later in 1892, Cleveland was elected to a second term. Cleveland is the only president to have served two terms that did not immediately follow one another. So Cleveland is the twenty-second and the twenty-fourth president, serving from 1885 to 1889 and from 1893 to 1897.

During Cleveland's second term, a serious depression hit the United States. Then the Cubans began fighting for their independence from Spain. Cleveland was urged to help the Cubans, but he refused. When American farmers in Hawaii tried to take over the government of that island, Cleveland wouldn't help them either. Cleveland didn't want to get mixed up in wars.

Cleveland was not very popular at the end of his second term. Many people blamed him for the bad economic times. They blamed him for not helping Cuba. Cleveland retired after leaving the White House to enjoy his big family until his death in 1908.

Recalling the Facts

Circle the correct ending to each of the following sentences. Then exchange papers with a partner to check your answers.

1. As a boy, Cleveland was a fine   (a) hunter   (b) fisherman   (c) mountain climber   (d) baseball player

2. Cleveland disliked working at the school for the blind because (a) it was far from home (b) the work was hard (c) the children were treated harshly (d) he couldn't teach

3. Cleveland served   (a) one term   (b) three terms   (c) four terms   (d) two terms that didn't follow each other

4. Cleveland was married while he was   (a) governor   (b) president   (c) sheriff   (d) still in college

5. When Cuba fought Spain, Cleveland   (a) did nothing   (b) sent troops   (c) sided with Spain   (d) went to Cuba

Individual Activities

MILITARY SPIRIT? A LETTER

Grover Cleveland was a young man during the Civil War, but he didn't serve. He did what many young men did: He paid for a substitute to take his place. Imagine that you are young Cleveland trying to explain this to a Civil War veteran. Write a letter to the veteran telling him why you didn't serve.

SCHOOL FOR THE BLIND: AN EXPOSÉ

Imagine you are a crusading reporter in 1852. You have seen the harsh conditions at the school for the blind. Write a news article describing all that is wrong.

IRISH AMERICANS STRIKE BACK: A JINGLE

The Irish Americans were very angry at James Blaine for the "rum, Romanism, and rebellion" slogan. Research Blaine and write a slogan attacking him. Create a slogan or jingle that the Irish-American supporters of Cleveland could have used.

BENJAMIN HARRISON

© 1967 by Dover Publications, Inc.

Young Ben Harrison was a slender, wiry boy. He was so blond that his hair was almost white. He loved to hunt, fish, and swim, but his favorite activity was school sports. He ran to school each day so he'd have a half hour before class started to play bullpen, an early type of baseball. The ball was made of India rubber, wrapped in yarn, then covered with leather by a shoemaker.

A bright boy, Ben read histories of Greece and Rome and biographies of great people. He enjoyed hearing his grandfather tell stories about the Indian wars. Ben often went to visit at his grandfather's farm—2000 acres of apple orchards, meadows, and trees.

Shortly before Ben's grandfather, William Henry Harrison, was elected president, Ben visited him in Cincinnati. As the boy walked down the street with his grandfather, he saw a fruit stand loaded with bright red apples. Ben filled his pockets. The woman selling apples screamed, "Thief!" Ben's grandfather quickly paid for the apples. He explained that his grandson was a farm boy, used to just taking apples!

Ben worried that once his grandfather moved into the White House, there would be no more big ham and chicken dinners at grandfather's house. He was right. Ben's grandfather died just one month after becoming president.

When he was fourteen, Ben had turned into a chubby, square-shouldered boy. He went to boarding school, and often got in trouble for wandering into fruit orchards with his friends and eating his fill of plums, cherries, and apples.

Born in North Bend, Ohio, in 1833, Ben Harrison became a lawyer in Indiana as a young man. He didn't make much money. He had to get an extra job as the town crier, a person who ran through town shouting the news of the day.

During the Civil War, Harrison commanded the 70th Indiana Infantry. He was a brave officer who was nicknamed "Little

Ben" by his soldiers, because he was 5 feet 6 inches tall.

Harrison was elected to the Senate after the war. He was not very popular because he didn't have a warm way with people. People who didn't like him said he was "as cold as an iceberg."

In 1888 Harrison was chosen by the Republicans to run for president. His grandfather had been president, and people joked about that. They said he wasn't a big enough man to wear his grandfather's hat. Many cartoons appeared in the papers showing a small Ben Harrison trying to fit into the giant hat worn by his grandfather.

Harrison became president. His wife, Caroline Lavinia, was a great help to him. She worked hard on many charities and was a fine watercolor artist. She started the White House collection of fine china and relics of past presidents.

Harrison had won the election by favoring high tariffs on foreign goods coming into the United States. He believed that if foreign-made goods were more costly, people would buy American-made goods. This would provide jobs for Americans.

Soon after Harrison became president, trouble broke out between the United States and Chile. The American ship U.S.S. *Baltimore* was visiting a port in Chile. One

hundred American sailors went ashore. A fight broke out between the sailors and some men from Chile. Two Americans were killed. Harrison was very angry. He seemed about to declare war against Chile over this. But the Chilean government said they were sorry, and they gave money to the families of the dead Americans.

Harrison got help for some men who had fought in the Civil War. He taxed goods from other countries as he had promised. But then the prices of food and clothing went up, and people didn't like that.

Harrison tried to help small farmers, especially in the West. They were having a hard time making it. Many of the farmers turned against the Republicans and the Democrats. They joined a new party that worked for farmers—the Populists.

When Harrison ran for a second term, he lost to Grover Cleveland, the man Harrison had defeated four years earlier. Harrison was the only grandson of a president to serve as president. He was president from 1889 to 1893.

Harrison returned to his law practice after leaving the White House. He also wrote a book about being president. An unpopular leader, he hadn't enjoyed being president. He died in 1901.

Recalling the Facts

Match each numbered description with one of the words or phrases below. Write the correct answer in the blank. Then exchange papers with a partner to check your answers.

tariffs   Indian wars   president   cold as an iceberg   Chile

1. Position Ben Harrison's grandfather held   _____

2. What Ben's grandfather told many stories about   _____

3. What some people called Harrison   _____

4. Country Ben Harrison considered going to war with   _____

5. High fees Harrison wanted   _____

Individual Activities

TOO SMALL: A CARTOON

Many cartoons made fun of Harrison as being too small to fill his grandfather's job. Some cartoons showed a little man under a huge hat. Make a cartoon using this idea. You can show someone trying to fill oversized shoes, peering over a big desk, trying to fill a big chair, etc. Use cartoon figures or stick figures. Or, describe the idea in one line.

STOLEN APPLES: A STORY OR POEM

Write a short story or a poem about young Ben grabbing the apple from the fruit stand in Cincinnati.

HARRISON FAMILY TREE

Make a family tree featuring the Harrison family. At the bottom of the page write: Benjamin Harrison (Caroline Lavinia Scott). Above those names write the names of Harrison's father and mother. Above those names write the names of Harrison's grandfather and grandmother.

WILLIAM McKINLEY

It was September 17, 1862, and the Civil War was going on. Young Sergeant Bill McKinley's job was passing out food to men and horses during the battle of Antietam Creek.

Sergeant McKinley was far away from home. He thought about the big white house in Poland, Ohio, where he grew up. He remembered the white picket fence and the maple trees. Those were happier days. But young Bill had wanted very much to fight in the Civil War. He hated slavery and he wanted to do his part to end it. That's why he had joined the army.

Now Bill had to drive his wagon into the smoke and fire of battle to bring fresh supplies to the weary soldiers on the front lines. Bill urged his mules to great speed. The soldiers watched the supply wagon come rumbling in. Hardly anybody could believe that the young driver lived through the fire of rifles and big guns. But Bill got the supplies safely through, and he was unhurt.

Sergeant McKinley delivered cooked rations of meat, coffee, and hard bread. From Bill's hands each soldier was served hot coffee and warm meats. This had never happened before in the regiment. The men had had to be content with cold, dry rations. For his act of bravery in coming through enemy fire to get the supplies to the front lines, Bill was promoted to second lieutenant. The brave young man now wore the golden shoulder straps of an officer in the Union Army.

Born in Niles, Ohio, in 1843, William McKinley became a teacher in a country school at seventeen. He walked three miles back and forth to school each day, leaping over fences as he went.

By the age of twenty, he had joined the army to fight in the Civil War. One of his commanders called McKinley "one of the bravest and finest officers in the army." At the end of the Civil War, McKinley became a lawyer and joined the Republican Party. In 1891, he was elected governor of Ohio. Five years later he became president of the United States.

McKinley favored full rights for all freed African-American slaves. He wanted all black males to have the right to vote. He wanted a better deal for American working people; he was against big business when it harmed workers. He wanted high taxes (tariffs) on goods from other countries to protect American jobs.

McKinley had to deal with a big problem in Cuba. The Cubans had been fighting for their independence from Spain. McKinley felt sorry for the Cubans, but he didn't want to get mixed up in their war with Spain.

In 1898 an American ship, the *Maine*, blew up while sitting in the harbor at Havana, Cuba. Two hundred and sixty Americans died on the *Maine*. Spain was immediately blamed for blowing up the ship, but they said they had nothing to do with it. Spanish soldiers in Cuba helped rescue Americans who had been wounded in the blast. But most Americans were sure the Spaniards had blown up the *Maine*. They demanded war right away.

"Remember the *Maine*!" was the battle cry. Newspapers printed stories of how Spain was abusing the Cubans. McKinley could no longer stand up against this war fury. Finally he agreed to go to war against Spain.

The Spanish-American War lasted four months. The United States won a big victory, gaining control of areas once owned by Spain. The U.S. now controlled Puerto Rico, Guam, and the Philippines. The U.S. had helped Cuba become independent from Spain. The war was very popular with the American people. But some Americans worried about what we would do with these new lands. Would we own them forever? Was it right that America would have an empire as England and Spain had once had?

McKinley also pushed trade with China during his presidency, and he promised a "full dinner pail" for all Americans. He was reelected to a second term in 1900.

On September 6, 1901, McKinley was visiting Buffalo, New York, when a man with a bandaged hand approached him. The always kindly McKinley got ready to shake the man's hand, not knowing that a gun was hidden under the fake bandages. Two shots rang out as Leon F. Czolgosz (pronounced CHAWL-gosh) gravely wounded the president. Czolgosz was a bitter man who hated all world leaders.

As McKinley was carried away, he begged that the man who shot him not be beaten. Eight days later, McKinley died. He had served as president from 1897 to 1901. He was the third American president to be assassinated.

Name _____ Date _____

Recalling the Facts

Place a check mark before each of the following jobs that McKinley held. Then exchange papers with a partner to check your answers.

_____ sailor	_____ governor
_____ soldier	_____ senator
_____ teacher	_____ lawyer
_____ police officer	_____ judge

Individual Activities

DR. WALTER REED: A MONUMENT

In 1900, an epidemic of yellow fever struck many American soldiers who were in Cuba after the Spanish-American War. The U.S. Army sent Dr. Walter Reed to Cuba to find the cause of the disease. Dr. Reed discovered that yellow fever was a virus transmitted through the bite of a mosquito.

Read about Dr. Reed in an encyclopedia or other source. Then, working with a partner, create a monument honoring Dr. Reed for what he did. Draw a picture of the monument or describe what it would look like.

PUERTO RICO AND GUAM: A REPORT

Puerto Rico and Guam were two of the territories the United States gained in the Spanish-American War. Draw a map and the flag of one of these territories. Write a paragraph describing the kind of government the territory has today.

PROSPERITY SLOGANS

During McKinley's campaign, his slogan was "four years more of the full dinner pail." We don't have dinner pails anymore. If a current president wanted to promise good times in a campaign, what words might be used? Write a modern slogan that promises prosperity—perhaps something like "a TV dinner in every microwave!"

THEODORE ROOSEVELT

©1967 by Dover Publications, Inc.

Young Theodore Roosevelt stood at the New York docks and stared at the large ship. "Teedie," as he was called by his family, said, "I know I won't like this trip."

The paddle-steamer *Scotia* left New York for Liverpool, England, in May of 1869. Teedie was a sickly boy who always had stomach trouble or colds. "I have a toothache in my stomach," he'd complain. His asthma was so bad that he had to sleep sitting up to be able to breathe. And now he was beginning a 377-day journey that would take him and his family across the ocean and then through Europe.

Teedie refused to join other young people in deck games. That bored him. Instead he struck up a friendship with a man from the West Indies who shared

Teedie's interest in natural history. Teedie had an amazing knowledge of animals. At home he counted the spots on garden spiders and recorded the information in his science notebooks. He kept detailed notes about all the animals he ever saw.

When the ship arrived in Europe, Teedie was determined not to let bad health spoil his adventures. He had entered into the spirit of the trip and he wanted to have fun. He walked all through Liverpool, England, visiting large houses and museums. In London he climbed up to the famous Tower, where many royal prisoners had been imprisoned and killed. Teedie climbed an 8000-foot mountain in the French Alps, rushed up the slopes of a volcano in Italy, and tossed pebbles into the bubbling lava. He met the Pope in Rome, and when finally the *Scotia* sailed for home, a group of whales sprayed the ship in farewell. Theodore Roosevelt had liked the trip after all.

Born in New York City in 1858, Theodore Roosevelt was an honors student at Harvard University. Because he'd worked hard as a boy to build up his weak body, he now enjoyed boxing, tennis, and other sports. He also read hundreds of books to develop his mind.

Roosevelt was elected to a government job in New York at the age of twenty-three, and he joined a group of other young men trying to make government better. They were called *reformers*. Roosevelt had just married Alice Hathaway Lee. In 1884, when Roosevelt was twenty-six, Alice died after giving birth to their first child, Alice. On the same day, Roosevelt was told that his mother had died. Roosevelt was so crushed by sorrow that he went west to live among cowboys and hunters.

Roosevelt wore thick glasses and had a New York accent, so the cowboys made fun of him when he first arrived. But one day a wild man threatened Roosevelt with two guns, and Roosevelt got the best of him. The cowboys changed their minds; soon Roosevelt was fitting in with rough western men.

When Roosevelt returned to New York two years later, he married Edith Kermit Carow. The family would eventually include six children, all of whom Roosevelt adored. Roosevelt became head of the New York Police Department. He walked the dangerous streets at night, learning all about police work. He found some dishonest men in the department and fired them.

When the Spanish-American War started, Roosevelt was eager to take part in it. But he was forty years old with poor eyesight. Still, he helped organize the First United States Volunteer Cavalry Regiment (the Rough Riders) and took command. After Roosevelt led his men up the hills of Cuba, he became famous all over America.

In 1900, Roosevelt was chosen vice president under McKinley. At McKinley's sudden death, forty-three-year-old Roosevelt became the youngest president in American history.

As president, Roosevelt declared war on those he called "the criminal rich." He called the White House a "bully pulpit." In that time "bully" meant excellent. Roosevelt loved the word, saying "bully for you!" when he wanted to praise somebody. He used his bully pulpit to attack large companies that banded together to fix prices and control trade.

Roosevelt also put in laws to make sure that meat was inspected and food and drugs were pure. He loved the outdoors himself and he wanted to protect it. He added millions of acres to the national forest. The number of national parks doubled under Roosevelt.

In 1905 Roosevelt was given the Nobel Peace Prize for helping end the Russo-Japanese War.

Roosevelt loved family life. He played with his children, dashing up hills and tumbling down the other side as if he were a child himself. At forty-six, he loved pillow fights and wild romping in the hayloft with his children. When away on trips, Roosevelt sent each child a letter containing drawings of every animal he saw.

In 1909, having been president since 1901, Roosevelt left the White House. He tried for the presidency again in 1912, running unsuccessfully as the Progressive—or Bull Moose—Party candidate. He then spent his time exploring the wilds of South America and Africa. The death of Roosevelt's youngest son, Quentin, during World War I broke his heart. He died eighteen months later in 1919, at sixty-one years old.

Recalling the Facts

Circle the correct ending to each of the following sentences. Then exchange papers with a partner to check your answers.

1. As a boy, Roosevelt went on   (a) an African safari   (b) a diving expedition   (c) a sea voyage   (d) a camping trip

2. Roosevelt led the Rough Riders in   (a) the Civil War   (b) World War I   (c) Indian wars   (d) the Spanish-American War

3. Roosevelt called the White House   (a) a pain   (b) useless   (c) a nightmare   (d) a bully pulpit

4. Roosevelt declared war on the   (a) criminal rich   (b) Cuba   (c) Bull Moose Party   (d) Russians

5. After leaving the White House, Roosevelt   (a) played golf   (b) wrote plays   (c) explored Africa and South America   (d) practiced law

Individual Activities

THE STAMP THAT ASSURES

Many Americans were sickened and killed by spoiled meat in the late 1800's. Roosevelt pressured Congress to pass the Meat Inspection Act to prevent this. A stamp on meat now tells us the government has inspected it. Imagine you were living in Roosevelt's time and got sick from bad, uninspected meat. Write a thank-you letter to the president, telling him what happened.

TEDDY BEARS: A STORY

Everybody knows what teddy bears are, but why are they called "teddy bears"? Do some research to find out. Write a story about how teddy bears got their name. Illustrate the story as Roosevelt might have done in letters to his children.

A VISIT TO A NATIONAL PARK: A REPORT

Crater Lake National Park (1902) and Mesa Verde National Park (1906) were both established under Theodore Roosevelt. Look up one of these parks in an encyclopedia or other source. Imagine you have visited the park, and write a report about it. Illustrate your report with drawings or with photocopied pictures.

WILLIAM HOWARD TAFT

©1967 by Dover Publications, Inc.

clothing, and the frightened horse kept galloping along, dragging the boy. Willie's head banged on the stones in the street.

When the carriage was finally stopped, Willie seemed to be dying. His head had to be sewn from ear to ear, leaving a lifelong scar. Willie's mother nursed him day and night. Slowly he recovered.

After the accident, Willie kept on growing. His friends called him Bill, but sometimes he was called Lub or Lubber because he was so big. He became a tough, determined boy, quick to smile but ready to fight when he had to. There were often fights between boys who lived in Bill's neighborhood and boys who lived in the Cincinnati flats called Butchertown. Once the Butchertown boys tried to beat up Bill's friends, but his flying fists drove them off.

Born in Cincinnati, Ohio, in 1857, William Howard Taft entered Yale University at age seventeen. He studied law, and in his spare time he boxed, wrestled, and rowed. His mother told him that someday he might become president of the United States, but that he wouldn't like it.

Willie Taft was born fat and healthy. He always wanted to be held in somebody's arms. At seven weeks old he had already grown out of his baby clothes. Willie had deep, dark-blue eyes and long, pretty curls, so everybody spoiled him.

Even though everybody in the family looked out for Willie, he had his share of accidents. When he was small, he picked up hot lumps of coal. When he was an older boy, he had an accident that almost killed him.

Willie was riding in a carriage when the horse suddenly went wild on a hill. Willie was thrown from the carriage as it turned over. The carriage wheels caught Willie's

Taft became a lawyer, then a judge. His father was a judge too, and young Taft loved the work. But when President McKinley asked him to become governor of the Philippines, Taft accepted. He was a fine governor who worried about the poor farmers and tried to provide land for them. He also built schools and roads and helped

Beyond the Cherry Tree: Stories of the Presidents

prepare the people for when they would become independent.

In 1904, Taft became Secretary of War. He led the building of the Panama Canal and became close friends with President Theodore Roosevelt. Then, even though he didn't want the job, he was talked into running for president in 1908 and won the election.

Although Roosevelt had urged Taft to run for president, their friendship ended when Taft was in the White House. Roosevelt had expected Taft to run the country exactly as he, Roosevelt, had done. He turned against Taft when that didn't happen.

Taft fired Gifford Pinchot, a popular forestry chief who was Roosevelt's friend. Roosevelt accused Taft of not caring about the wilderness.

Taft started the Postal Savings System so people could safely save money. He continued to stop big business from fixing prices, just as Roosevelt had done. But Taft was not a popular president. He was, as his mother had predicted long ago, unhappy in the job. Taft wanted to go off and play golf instead of sitting at his desk solving problems. He disliked all the quarreling that went on in politics. Taft wanted a peaceful, happy life—and he couldn't have that as president.

In 1912 Taft had to run for reelection because the Republican Party expected it. Theodore Roosevelt was now Taft's biggest enemy, so Roosevelt decided he'd run for president too, on the Progressive Party ticket. The election of 1912 became a three-way match between Taft, Roosevelt, and Woodrow Wilson in the Democratic Party. Taft and Roosevelt split the Republican vote, so the election went to Woodrow Wilson. Taft left the White House having served from 1909 to 1913.

In 1921, Taft got the job he had always wanted. He became Chief Justice of the Supreme Court. The final ten years of his life were the happiest. He had always enjoyed being a judge, and now he had risen as high as a judge could rise. Taft was so happy being on the Supreme Court that he said, "I don't even remember that I ever was president!" Taft died in 1930.

Name _____ Date _____

Recalling the Facts

In the list below, check off the jobs Taft held during his life. Then exchange papers with a partner to check your answers.

1. lawyer _____   5. governor _____

2. judge _____   6. forestry chief _____

3. farmer _____

4. teacher _____

Individual Activities

CHERRY BLOSSOM TIME: A PAINTING

Taft's wife, Helen Herron Taft, arranged for the cherry blossoms which now bloom in Washington, D.C. They were a gift from the Japanese government. Find a photograph of cherry blossoms. Using it as a guide, paint or draw the Washington cherry blossoms. Or write a letter to the Japanese government telling them how beautiful their gift has become.

GIFFORD PINCHOT

Gifford Pinchot did a lot to save America's forests, but most people never heard of him. Theodore Roosevelt hired him and Taft fired him. Look up Pinchot and, with the help of a partner, design a monument for him. Either draw a picture of the monument or describe it. (Hint: What did Pinchot like more than anything? What sort of a monument does this suggest?)

PRESIDENTS AND RECREATION

Taft loved to play golf. It was popular in the circles he traveled in. What sports do adults in your neighborhood enjoy? Ask adult relatives or friends about what sports they enjoy. If they were elected president, would they play basketball instead of golf? Keep a record of answers, and write them in a survey to bring to class.

WOODROW WILSON

©1967 by Dover Publications, Inc.

Thomas Woodrow Wilson was called Tommy as he was growing up. The son and grandson of a long line of ministers, Tommy loved books, but he was afraid he was the slowest reader in the world. He was nine years old before he learned the alphabet, and eleven before he could read fairly well. But even then, he was slow in reading and understanding what he was reading.

Tommy knew his parents were ashamed of how slow he was. When people mentioned Tommy's problem, his parents became upset. That made the boy try harder than ever, but he couldn't understand what was wrong with him. Some now think that young Wilson had a reading disorder that made letters appear to him in the wrong order.

To overcome his problem, Tommy trained himself to study very hard. He improved his memory and taught himself how to write quickly so he could take notes in class and study them over and over later.

Tom Wilson's most important teacher was his father. He not only taught the boy history and other subjects, but he took him everywhere so he could see firsthand how the world ran. Father and son visited machine shops and furnace boilers. Tom stared wide-eyed at huge engines clanging and watched sheets of flame dancing from the roaring furnaces. Tom's father wanted his son to know how hard people worked to keep America going. Tom gained a deep respect for working people from these experiences.

Born in Staunton, Virginia, in 1856, Woodrow Wilson studied law at Princeton University. He then got a degree in political science and wrote a hook about government. For twelve years he taught about the government and wrote articles and books. Wilson then became president of Princeton, but he didn't enjoy the job because of all the quarreling among the teachers.

Wilson entered politics and became governor of New Jersey in 1910. He made many improvements in the state. He put in fairer elections, an insurance plan for injured workers, and many other good laws. His success as governor made him well known all over America. When he ran for president in 1912, he was elected partly because it was a three-way race.

As president, Wilson put in a plan called the New Freedom. He wanted to lower taxes on goods from other countries. He favored free world trade. He favored stopping child labor, and he wanted an eight-hour working day. Wilson wanted to make it easier for farmers to get loans.

Wilson was a strong, hardworking president. He wanted to solve the problems of the American people at home, but world problems got in the way of his plans. World War I was raging in Europe, and Wilson wanted to stay out of it. He hoped the war could be ended by peace talks.

In 1915, German submarines sank a British ship, the *Lusitania.* One thousand passengers died, including many women and children—even babies. One hundred and twenty-four of the dead were Americans. Cries of anger rose up all across America. Many people wanted Wilson to immediately declare war on Germany, but he refused. In 1916 he ran for reelection on the slogan "He kept us out of war." Although many Americans wanted war to punish Germany for the loss of the *Lusitania,* many more Americans dreaded the thought of war and losing their loved ones in the fighting. So the majority of people voted for Wilson, believing he would keep America out of World War I.

In April 1917, at the beginning of Wilson's second term, there was more trouble with Germany. Wilson decided to go to war after all. America joined with Britain, France, and Russia to form the Allies. They fought against Germany.

After about a year and a half, 116,000 Americans had died in the war, and many more were wounded. But peace finally came when the Allies won. Wilson hoped this war was "the war to end all wars." He helped start the League of Nations, a group of nations that was supposed to settle problems so that wars wouldn't break out anymore.

Wilson traveled all over the world and the United States making speeches for the League of Nations. He wanted all nations to join. But many Americans were afraid that if the United States joined the League, then we would be mixed up in the troubles of the world. In the end, Wilson could not get the United States Congress to agree to join the League of Nations.

During his fight to save the League, Wilson suffered a stroke. During his long illness and his wife, Edith Bolling Wilson, was his nurse and companion. In many ways she helped run the White House. Wilson left office in 1921, having served from 1913 to 1921. He won the Nobel Peace Prize, but he lost his dream for a League of Nations with the United States in it. Wilson died in 1924, a sad man.

Recalling the Facts

Circle the correct ending to each of the following sentences. Then exchange papers with a partner to check your answers.

1. As a boy Wilson had trouble with   (a) arithmetic   (b) sports   (c) reading   (d) many sick spells

2. Wilson's most important teacher was his   (a) mother   (b) older sister   (c) uncle   (d) father

3. Wilson's program was called the   (a) Fair Deal   (b) Square Deal   (c) New Freedom   (d) Lands Deal

4. The *Lusitania* was   (a) American   (b) French   (c) German   (d) British

5. Wilson left office   (a) satisfied   (b) angry at politics   (c) sad over the League of Nations   (d) content and happy

ELECTION OF 1912: A MATH PROBLEM

Look in an encyclopedia to find out how many popular votes Wilson, Taft, and Roosevelt got. Add up the Taft and Roosevelt votes. Then answer this question, based on the figures: If Roosevelt hadn't run and all the Republicans had voted for Taft, who would have been elected president in 1912? Prove it.

THE TERRIBLE WEAPONS OF WORLD WAR I

Many new and deadly weapons were introduced in World War I. Choose the airplane, submarine, tank, or machine gun for a project. Research the weapon you chose. Draw a picture of it, or photocopy the picture from a book. Then describe why this weapon was so effective.

THE TRENCHES

The soldiers of World War I lived in water-filled trenches infested with rats and insects. Research what life was like there. Then imagine you are a soldier during World War I. Write a letter home explaining what it's like.

WARREN G. HARDING

©1967 by Dover Publications, Inc.

As a boy, Warren Harding worked at a sawmill making brooms. Then he drove a team of horses for the Toledo and Ohio Central Railroad. He milked cows, painted barns, and planted wheat. He even tried teaching, but he said that was the hardest job of all. He worked for a small newspaper setting type and washing printing-press rollers. He liked that. Warren didn't enjoy working at so many jobs, but he liked money.

As Warren grew older, it was time to decide what he'd do in life. His mother wanted him to study to be a minister, but Warren didn't feel called to that. He didn't want to be a lawyer either.

Then nineteen-year-old Warren thought he had found the perfect job. He and two young friends sat at Reilly's Beefsteak Palace on Main Street in Marion, Ohio, one day in 1884. The large, friendly eyes of Warren lit up as he said, "We can buy the *Marion Star* for $300 cash and a loan." The other two young men shrugged. Everybody knew the paper was in trouble. The presses were old and the paper was in debt. Marion already had two newspapers; maybe that was enough.

"Listen," said Warren, "the town can support another paper. Lots of rich farmers live in town. The railroad is growing. When I was a young kid, I worked for the little *Caledonia Argus*. I can find news. I can get ads. I know my way around the printing press."

Warren's friends finally agreed. The tall, warm teenager turned the *Marion Star* into a big success. His own future was off to a good start.

Warren Harding was born in Corsica, Ohio, in 1865. He was the well-liked newspaper editor of the *Marion Star* when he turned to politics. He was elected to government jobs as a Republican; then he became a U.S. senator.

Harding wasn't interested in higher office, but his wife, Florence, saw a bright future for her husband in politics. She urged him to reach for the top. Friends said that the handsome Harding "looked like a president." And before long, Harding was on his way to *becoming* president.

In 1920 Harding was chosen to be the Republican candidate for president. After World War I, Americans longed to return to peace and good times. Harding's slogan was "Back to Normalcy," and that sounded good to many voters. He was elected president.

People trusted and liked Harding because he seemed like a nice, friendly man. Harding said he knew he could never be the best president America had ever had, but he wanted to be the best-loved president. When the Hardings moved into the White House, they acted like common people. They opened up the White House to visitors, and they often joined American visitors to chat in the hall. People were amazed to be actually talking to the president and his wife.

Harding chose some good people for his cabinet. He chose Herbert Hoover to be Secretary of Commerce and Charles Evans Hughes as Secretary of State. But Harding also chose some people who were unfit for government service. They were old friends of Harding, and they were dishonest and greedy men.

In a short time, some of Harding's men were stealing from the government. Secretary of the Interior Albert Fall took money from private companies in exchange for renting them government oil lands. This was called the Teapot Dome scandal. The oil was in Teapot Dome, Wyoming. Attorney General Daugherty was mixed up in crooked deals. There was so much stealing going on that Harding's team was called the "Ohio Gang."

Harding began to see that all was not well. He said, "I have no trouble with my enemies, but my friends are keeping me walking the floor nights."

Colonel Forbes, who ran the Veterans Administration, gained money from selling leftover war supplies. Another of Harding's men died of a gunshot wound to the head. Many people thought he had something to hide and could not face going to prison.

President Harding was very upset by all this. He decided to take a trip to Alaska to forget his troubles. On the trip he became ill with food poisoning, and then he appeared to have a stroke. Harding died on August 2, 1923, having served as president from 1921 to 1923. Most Americans were very sad to hear of the president's sudden death. They didn't yet know about all the crooked deals going on at the White House—but they soon found out.

Recalling the Facts

Mark a minus sign (–) after each statement that describes something Harding shouldn't have done. Mark a plus sign (+) after each statement that describes something Harding did right. Then exchange papers with a partner to check your answers.

1. Harding bought the *Marion Star.* _____

2. Harding became a U.S. senator. _____

3. Harding chose Albert Fall for Secretary of the Interior. _____

4. Harding chose Herbert Hoover as Secretary of Commerce. _____

5. Harding chose Colonel Forbes as head of the Veterans Administration. _____

Individual Activities

HARDING'S OBITUARY

Warren G. Harding did many successful things. As a newspaper editor, he wrote many obituaries for famous people. Imagine you are a friend of Harding and you must write his obituary. Read some obituaries in the newspaper; notice that they mostly tell good things. Write an obituary stressing Harding's good points.

HARDING'S DEATH: A MYSTERY

Early reports of Harding's illness said he had pneumonia. Then the newspaper reports said he was sick from spoiled crabmeat. Then they said he died of uremic (kidney) poisoning or a stroke. Look into at least four books about Harding and write down what they say about his final illness. Then write a paragraph giving your opinion about what he died of.

HARDING AS NEWSPAPERMAN

Imagine that Warren Harding remained as editor of the *Marion Star* or became editor of a bigger newspaper. Would that have been better for him and for the country? Explain in one paragraph.

CALVIN COOLIDGE

©1967 by Dover Publications, Inc.

Red-haired Calvin Coolidge was raised in Plymouth Notch, a small Vermont town. The boy was up at dawn in a room without heat. He washed in cold water and then went out to fill the family wood box with chopped wood.

Calvin's job was to lead the cattle out to the meadow in the summer and feed them in winter. He cared for the chickens and hogs, fixed fences, plowed the fields, and sold apples and popcorn balls at the town meetings—all to help the family.

Young Calvin's biggest problem was shyness. He struggled with this all his life. Calvin always seemed to be suffering from a cold, too, and this made his strange, quacking voice sound worse. This made his shyness worse too. Every time he opened his mouth, he thought he sounded awful, so he tried to avoid speaking to strangers. When Calvin got home and heard strange voices in his house, he felt frightened. He knew he'd have to make polite talk to people he didn't know. The hardest thing he ever did was walk into the house at such times to face strangers.

Calvin worried about his shyness. He feared it would keep him from being successful in life. So he forced himself to make new friends. He took a part-time job making toys and baby carriages, but he never did make a close friend. He spent all his free time with his sister, Abbie.

Little by little, though, Calvin rose above his shyness. He learned to get along quite well in the world.

Born in Vermont in 1872, Calvin Coolidge became a lawyer as a young man. He was extremely thrifty, saving every spare penny he made. He refused to buy a car or a home of his own. He refused to go into debt for anything.

In 1898 Coolidge became a city councilman. Then he worked his way up in the Republican Party. By 1915 he was the lieutenant governor of Massachusetts. Three years later he was governor. In this job Coolidge gained the attention of the entire country.

On September 19, 1919, the police department of Boston, Massachusetts, went on strike. They wanted more pay, a better pension system, and fairer working conditions. But with the police on strike, the people of Boston had no protection. Young gangs roamed the streets, smashing car windows. They threw stones at passengers as they ran from the stopped trolleys. The plate-glass windows of stores were smashed in. Unruly, shouting crowds stole everything in sight. Wild mobs took over. At this point, Governor Coolidge called out the state guard to bring back order. Coolidge said of the striking police, "There is no right to strike against the public safety by anybody, anywhere, anytime." This statement caught the attention of the nation. Coolidge became a hero.

At the 1920 Republican convention, Coolidge's successful handling of the Boston police strike was remembered. He seemed the perfect choice to run with Harding. The Harding-Coolidge ticket won a big victory.

When Harding died, Coolidge was visiting his father in Vermont. Coolidge's own father, a notary public, swore him in as president. Then Coolidge hurried back to Washington to become president.

Coolidge and his wife, Grace Goodhue Coolidge, moved into the White House. Mrs. Coolidge had worked hard as a teacher of the deaf all her life. She was a kindly woman who was soon voted one of America's most admired women.

Americans at first felt sad over Harding's sudden death. But then they were shocked when stories of the dishonesty of his administration came out. Coolidge had a big job cleaning up the mess. The very honest—and almost grimly serious—Coolidge was perfect for the role. He did his job well and brought back trust in the honesty of the government. In 1924, when Coolidge ran for reelection, he won a big victory with the slogan "Keep cool with Coolidge."

Coolidge stood for common sense and thrift. He cut government spending and lowered taxes. The country enjoyed good times with plenty of jobs. But wages were low, and the farmers had a terrible time making a living. On the surface, the American economy looked fine, but a little deeper look revealed trouble ahead.

Coolidge was not interested in world problems. He thought government should do as little as possible. He believed that people should run their own lives and that the government should get out of the way of business. "The business of America is business," he said. In 1928 Coolidge was still popular, but he wouldn't run again. "I do not choose to run," he said simply but firmly. He had served from 1923 to 1929. He returned to a quiet private life until his death in 1933.

Recalling the Facts

Calvin Coolidge had an unusual personality. Beside each statement that accurately describes him, mark a plus sign (+). Beside each statement that doesn't describe him, mark a minus sign (−).

1. He was a friendly man, always telling fine jokes. _____

2. He would not waste a single coin on anything. _____

3. He thought any working person had the right to strike. _____

4. He was strictly honest in every way. _____

5. He had an unpleasant voice and was shy. _____

Individual Activities

WAYS TO SELF-RESPECT: A POSTER

Coolidge said there were two ways to have self-respect: "To spend less than you make and to make more than you spend." Print this quotation on a poster, and then choose a photograph or cartoon that fits it. Use your imagination. It can be anything from a credit card with a line through it to a smiling face of a debt-free person.

A GREAT MAN? AN OPINION

Calvin Coolidge said that every president should know that "he is not a great man." Write in one paragraph what you think he meant by this. Do you agree?

COOLIDGE: A CARTOON

To lighten his image as a grim, serious man, Coolidge sometimes put on unusual hats, like cowboy hats or Indian warbonnets. Create a cartoon by photo-copying a picture of Coolidge and drawing an unusual hat on his head. Then write a suitable caption for the cartoon.

HERBERT HOOVER

©1967 by Dover Publications, Inc.

Herbert Hoover had a truly merry early childhood. His father was a small-town inventor, and young Herbert enjoyed tinkering in his father's workshop. Bert, his older brother, and his younger sister lived in a small cottage on Wapsinonoc Creek in Iowa. The house was surrounded by flowers and fruit trees. The children made maple sugar eggs and picked bright red Siberian crabapples. Then, when Bert was six, his father died. Three years later his mother died. The three Hoover children were orphans.

"We were orphans three," wrote Bert's brother, "Bert and I and little Marie." The children were sent away to different relatives who offered to take them.

Bert rode a Union Pacific train bound for his Uncle John's farm in Oregon. He stared out the train window and wondered about his future.

Uncle John didn't believe that young people should have easy lives. He believed they should work hard. Bert had to work eleven hours a day chopping wood and cleaning the forest of fir trees. At night the boy had scary dreams of being attacked by armies of tall trees.

"I do not think Bert was very happy," Uncle John recalled later. "Our home was not like the one he left behind with his parents in it." Uncle John noted that in his parents' home Bert had almost no work.

Because of the constant hard work, Bert looked older than he was. He always walked with his gaze fixed on the ground. Uncle John was right. Bert wasn't happy.

Born in West Branch, Iowa, in 1874, Herbert Hoover had a rough childhood as an orphan. As a teenager he worked all day and studied mathematics at night. He wanted to join the first class at the new Stanford University in California and become a mining engineer.

Hoover came to be called the boy wonder of engineering. At the age of twenty-three, he ran gold mines in Australia. For the next fifteen years he worked on engineering projects in Europe, India, South Africa, and Egypt. He also wrote an important book called *Principles of Mining*. Hoover married Lou Henry, a geology major, and she helped him translate a rare mining book from Latin to English. Lou Henry Hoover, as bright as her husband, was the first woman to graduate from Stanford in geology. She kept a lifelong interest in the Girl Scout movement.

When Hoover was forty years old, he had already made enough money to allow him to stop working. He spent much of his time doing good works. During and after World War I, he helped starving war refugees. He figured out ways to get food and clothing to 300,000,000 people. Hoover's work made him a beloved figure throughout the world.

Hoover became Secretary of Commerce in Harding's administration. Then, in 1928, he was chosen by the Republicans to run for president. He seemed like a brilliant, wonderful man who had risen above a grim childhood to become rich and generous as well. That year the Democrats chose Alfred E. Smith as their candidate. He was a Catholic, and many Americans didn't want to vote for a Catholic. All the American presidents before this had been Protestants. Hoover won an easy victory.

When Hoover ran for president, his campaign slogan was "a chicken in every pot." Times seemed good in America; few people saw the signs of trouble in the economy. Farmers were losing money, and Americans were buying stocks by paying just a little bit down and owing the rest. When the price of stocks fell, the people could lose everything.

Soon after Hoover took office, the worst depression in American history began. The stock market crashed on October 24, 1929. Thousands of Americans lost all their money. This was only the beginning of a disaster. Soon businesses were closing; millions of people lost their jobs. Factories closed and banks failed. Prices dropped and people lost their homes.

Hoover tried to deal with all this, but things kept getting worse. The numbers of angry, jobless Americans grew. People who lost their homes moved into neighborhoods of sheds and called them "Hoovervilles." People wrapped themselves in newspapers and called them "Hoover blankets." Hoover was blamed for everything.

Hoover had once been poor, but by his own effort he had become rich. He believed that if everyone worked hard, the Depression would end. He kept promising good times just around the corner, but they never came. In 1932, Hoover lost his try for reelection, after serving from 1929 to 1933.

Hoover returned to private life, doing good works like helping refugees from World War II and improving government efficiency. He died at age ninety in 1964.

Recalling the Facts

Circle the correct ending to each of the following sentences. Then exchange papers with a partner to check your answers.

1. Hoover had sadness in his childhood because he   (a) was poor   (b) lost his parents   (c) failed school   (d) was sickly

2. Hoover's Uncle John believed children should   (a) have fun   (b) work hard   (c) travel   (d) learn piano

3. Hoover was a successful   (a) mining engineer   (b) lawyer   (c) farmer   (d) lumber mill owner

4. Hoovervilles were   (a) shed towns   (b) mining camps   (c) White House toys   (d) college rooms

5. Hoover wasn't reelected because of   (a) World War I   (b) World War II   (c) the Depression   (d) dishonest friends

Individual Activities

ADVICE TO THE YOUNG: A POSTER

Hoover's advice to the young was this: "Be honest, be sportsmanlike, be considerate of others, have religious faith, and be educated." Make a poster that includes all or part of this advice. On your poster include a drawing or photograph that illustrates the advice.

LETTER FROM UNCLE JOHN'S

Imagine you are young Bert Hoover facing another day of cutting down trees. Write a letter home to an old friend on Wapsinonoc Creek telling about your life now.

THE STOCK MARKET CRASH: STOCKS TODAY

Look at the financial section of your daily newspaper and find the stock market reports. Find any stock and write down the price of one share. Follow this stock for a week. Imagine you have bought five shares. Figure out at the end of the week if you have lost or gained money. Do this with a partner who chooses a different stock. Compare your successes or failures.

FRANKLIN DELANO ROOSEVELT

©1967 by Dover Publications, Inc.

Young Franklin Roosevelt was on a trip to Washington with his father, James Roosevelt. They visited the White House because President Grover Cleveland was a friend of the family. Cleveland was having a hard time just then. As the Roosevelts were about to leave, Cleveland leaned close to Franklin and said, "I have just one wish for you. Pray to God that He will never let you be president of the United States!"

The last thing on Franklin's mind was being president. He was an only child living at a huge house called Springwood on 1000 acres. There were beautiful lawns, grapevines, flower gardens, and many animals. Franklin enjoyed his goats, dogs,

and horses, but his favorite pet was a pony named Debbie.

Franklin was the prince of Springwood, exploring the woods, learning every rock and tree. He built a grand tree house overlooking the Hudson River and pretended to be a pirate. Franklin's mother loved him very much and wanted to be with him all the time.

At age fourteen, Franklin had his own sailboat. His father hired a sea captain to teach Franklin how to sail the twenty-one-foot boat, the *New Moon*. Franklin sailed from Maine to Canada, learning the reefs and how to manage the wind and trim his sails. He had become a fine young sailor.

Born in Hyde Park, New York, in 1882, Franklin Roosevelt had been to Europe eight times before he was fifteen. He and his family often traveled around the United States in a private railroad car with all the comforts of home. At Harvard University, the 6-foot-tall, 140-pound Roosevelt was an average student and a poor athlete.

After college, Roosevelt became a lawyer and soon was rising in the Democratic Party. Well liked with a big smile, Roosevelt married a distant cousin, Eleanor Roosevelt, in 1905. Eleanor's uncle, former President Theodore Roosevelt, gave the bride away. Five children were born to the Roosevelts. At thirty-nine, when Roosevelt was planning his political future, he was suddenly stricken with polio. He was desperately ill for a while and lost the use of his legs. He couldn't even move his toes for months, and he struggled to regain his health. He could never again walk without leg braces, a cane, or someone to lean on, but he drove a car with special hand controls.

During all his suffering, Roosevelt developed the strength that would someday make him a great man. With tremendous moral support from Eleanor Roosevelt, Roosevelt returned to politics. He was elected governor of New York in 1929. In 1932 he was elected president of the United States.

When Roosevelt became president, America was in the middle of a terrible depression. Millions were jobless, home-less, and hungry, and they had just about lost hope. The new president promised a New Deal for the American people. He said "You have nothing to fear but fear itself." With his big, booming, friendly voice, he encouraged the people during radio talks called Fireside Chats. Roosevelt changed the way America worked. He gave direct help to the poor, and he set up many different programs to meet various needs. Because of all the letters in the short versions of their names, these programs were nicknamed "alphabet soup." The WPA gave government jobs to the jobless, AAA helped farmers, CCC helped jobless youth,

the FDIC made sure money in the bank was safe, and the NRA helped to get business going again.

One of Roosevelt's most important programs was Social Security. For the first time in American history, aged and disabled Americans would get a monthly pension.

During this time, Eleanor Roosevelt traveled 40,000 miles meeting people. Roosevelt called her his "eyes." She was responsible for many of the laws that eased the suffering of the people.

During this time in Europe, an evil madman named Adolf Hitler was taking over many countries. He wanted to take over the world with the help of his allies, Italy and Japan. Roosevelt sent help to Great Britain and France as they tried desperately to stop Hitler.

In December 1941, Japan bombed Pearl Harbor. The United States joined in World War II. Roosevelt led the nation during four years of war. He was reelected four times, serving from 1933 to 1945. In April of 1945 Roosevelt died in office, just months before peace came.

Roosevelt made government responsi-ble for the good of the people. Many loved him; others said he made government too big. He was the president during America's worst crisis since the Civil War.

Recalling the Facts

Following is a list of events that occurred during Franklin Roosevelt's life. The events are out of order. In the blanks before the sentences, number the events in the correct order. Exchange papers with a partner to check your answers.

(a) _____ Roosevelt was elected governor of New York.

(b) _____ Roosevelt was elected president for the fourth time.

(c) _____ Roosevelt married Eleanor Roosevelt.

(d) _____ Japan bombed Pearl Harbor.

(e) _____ Roosevelt was stricken with polio.

Individual Activities

FIRST LADY OF THE WORLD

Eleanor Roosevelt came to be called the First Lady of the World because of her work helping Americans through the Depression, and also because of her social welfare work throughout the world. Research Eleanor Roosevelt and think of what might be an appropriate way to honor her. For example, you could design a monument or write a paragraph in tribute.

ROOSEVELT MEMORIAL

In 1993, work was begun on a Roosevelt Memorial. Franklin Roosevelt will only be the fourth president so honored. He will join Washington, Lincoln, and Jefferson in West Potomac Park. Research what this monument will look like and photocopy pictures of the design. Write why you think Roosevelt was chosen for this high honor.

WHAT IS THE FDIC?

Visit your neighborhood bank and look for a notice mentioning the FDIC. Then ask one of the bank employees what FDIC means. Write a brief report on what you have learned.

Harry S Truman

©1967 by Dover Publications, Inc.

Harry Truman was small for his age and always seemed to be in trouble. Harry once almost choked on a peach pit. One year, he was so sick that he couldn't walk for a while. His mother had to wheel him around in a baby carriage. Harry had weak eyes and had to wear thick glasses.

But when Harry wasn't sick, he had a good time on his parents' 600-acre farm. Harry had a black Shetland pony of his own to ride, a Maltese cat named Bob, and a tan dog named Tandy.

As a young teenager, Harry got a job mopping and sweeping at the local drugstore in Independence, Missouri. Then, in 1901, he tried for his first real job. He was a thin seventeen-year-old who still wore thick glasses. Someone was needed as a time-keeper on the railroad. The timekeeper had to keep records for 400 laborers and pay them as well. Could a weak-looking boy like Harry handle the tough railroaders?

Harry told the boss, L.J. Smith, that he could do the job—and he got it. Soon Harry was working ten hours a day, six days a week, for $1.50 a day. He slept in the railroad tents, and he brought the weekly wages to rough-and-tumble saloons where the railroad men went after work.

Harry did the job of timekeeper well. He learned a lot about handling different kinds of people too. That would be a big help in the future, when he commanded soldiers and entered politics.

Born in Lamar, Missouri, in 1884, Harry Truman never went to college, because he had to go to work early in life. He was a bank clerk, farmer, and owner of a store that sold men's clothing. Then, during World War I, Truman commanded a field unit. After the war he was elected judge, and his political life began.

In 1934 Truman became a United States senator. During World War II, he made sure that money wasn't being wasted in the war effort. Truman's success here caught the eye of President Roosevelt, who chose Truman for vice president in 1944.

At the news that Roosevelt had died, Truman said to some reporters, "Boys . . . if you ever pray, pray for me now. Yesterday

I felt like the moon, the stars, and all the planets had fallen on me!"

The new president brought World War II to an end. He ordered atomic bombs to be dropped on two Japanese cities, Hiroshima and Nagasaki. This forced Japan to give up. Many soldiers' lives on both sides were saved, but Truman had taken a very serious step. The atomic bomb was a truly terrible weapon, and it had never been used before. About 150,000 people died in those two Japanese cities.

In 1948, Truman ran for president himself. Many people thought he would lose to Tom Dewey, the Republican candidate, but Truman won in a close election.

Truman was faced with the rise of Communism in the world and the beginning of what was called the Cold War. During World War II, the United States and the Soviet Union (Russia) had been friends and allies. But now, after the war, the Communist Soviet Union took over countries in Eastern Europe and seemed about to take over most of the world. The Cold War was the struggle of the free, non-Communist world to keep Communism from spreading. Truman gave massive help to Western Europe, Greece, and Turkey to make sure Communism wouldn't take over there.

During Truman's term, there was a revolution in China, and Communism took over. China had been an ally of the United States during World War II. Now it was an ally of the Soviet Union. North Korea, another Communist country, attacked our friend, South Korea. The Chinese Communists helped North Korea. Truman sent American troops to help South Korea under the flag of the United Nations.

The Korean War cost the lives of thousands of Americans. Truman's popularity fell, and he did not run for reelection in 1952. The American people were tired of the Korean War; they wanted to bring the troops home. Truman had served as president from 1945 to 1953.

Truman returned to Independence, Missouri, where he lived quietly for twenty more years. When he was president, Truman often said, "The buck stops here." He was never afraid to make tough decisions and stick with them. The American people respected him for that. Truman died in 1972.

Recalling the Facts

Circle the correct ending to each of the following sentences. Then exchange papers with a partner to check your answers.

1. At seventeen, Truman was a   (a) cook   (b) timekeeper   (c) farmer   (d) lawyer

2. Truman owned a store that sold   (a) hardware   (b) feed   (c) men's clothing
   (d) groceries

3. When Roosevelt died, Truman said   (a) "I'll do fine."   (b) "No problem."
   (c) "I can't handle the job."   (d) "Pray for me."

4. Truman gave money to war-damaged countries to stop   (a) Hitler   (b) Communism
   (c) China   (d) Japan

5. The war that took place while Truman was president was   (a) World War I
   (b) the Korean War   (c) the Vietnam War   (d) the Spanish-American War

Individual Activities

PLAIN TALK: IN TRUMAN'S WORDS

Truman was a plainspoken man. Read some books about Truman and find some quotes. Notice how he spoke in clear, simple English. Write down some of his comments. Then, in one paragraph, give your opinion of his way of speaking.

MOTTOS: A CARTOON

Truman liked to say, "The buck stops here." Sometimes he said, "If you can't stand the heat, stay out of the kitchen." Choose a cartoon or make a drawing that fits either of these sayings.

WHY DEWEY LOST

Read about the election of 1948. Everybody thought Dewey would win. Find some answers in several books about why he lost. Then, in one paragraph, write your own opinion.

Dwight D. Eisenhower

©1967 by Dover Publications, Inc.

As a boy, Dwight Eisenhower, nick-named Ike, lived on three acres in a big two-story house. Ike did chores like all the other farm boys, milking the cows, water-ing the horses, and collecting eggs. Ike and his brothers each had a garden where they raised vegetables to sell to the neighbors. Ike grew sweet corn and cucumbers on his patch.

When Ike was very small, he went to visit his Aunt Minnie in Topeka, Kansas. He was having a fine time exploring the back-yard until a huge goose came at him, hiss-ing and flapping its wings. Ike ran inside and asked his uncle to remove the goose, but his uncle handed the boy a broom and told him to settle the quarrel with the goose by himself. Young Ike grabbed the broom and ran toward the goose with a wild yell, giving the bird a whack. From then on, Ike ruled the backyard.

Ike had a very bad temper as a boy. Once his father refused to let him go trick-or-treating with his older brothers. Ike flew into a rage and began beating his fists on the trunk of an old apple tree until his hands were bloody. Ike's father cut a switch from a tree and whipped the boy, then sent him to bed. An hour later Ike's mother heard the boy still sobbing. She told him it was up to him right now to control his temper or it would control him. Ike looked at his bloody, bruised hands and agreed. From then on he never had such an awful rage.

Born in Denison, Texas, in 1890, Dwight Eisenhower worked at a dairy as a teenager. He dreamed of going to college, but his parents couldn't afford to send him. So, to get a free education, Eisenhower joined the army and went to school at West Point.

Eisenhower trained men to fight in World War I, but it was World War II that made him famous. In 1942 Eisenhower was chosen to command American forces in Europe. Eisenhower did a good job and was then given command of all Allied forces. In 1943 he became a four-star general; his forces defeated one of the Axis powers, Italy. Then Eisenhower led the invasion of France on D-Day. As Supreme Commander, Eisenhower defeated Germany and accepted their surrender on May 7, 1945.

After the war, Eisenhower came home as a great hero. Hardly anybody in the country was not familiar with the soldier's big, confident smile. He became president of Columbia University, but both the Republicans and the Democrats wanted him as their candidate for president. The cry "I like Ike" was heard all over America.

In 1952, America was stuck in an unpopular war in Korea. People were looking for someone to lead the country back to peace. Eisenhower became the Republican candidate for president. He promised to go to Korea and try to make peace if he was elected.

Eisenhower won a huge victory and ended the Korean War soon after he became president. A kindly, fatherly figure with a warm, motherly wife, Mamie Doud Eisenhower, Eisenhower won the hearts of most Americans. He was president during a peaceful and happy time in American history. The young soldiers from World War II and the Korean War had come home. Now they were buying houses and cars and raising families. The Cold War was going on between the free world and the Communist world, but it was not a shooting war; there were no casualties. For eight years people enjoyed peace and good economic times.

Eisenhower spent a lot of money on national defense so the free world could hold its own against the Communists. But he hated spending so much on the military.

In 1954 the Supreme Court decided that all children, whatever their color, had to go to school together. For many years in the South, white and black children had gone to separate schools by law. After the Supreme Court decision, some white parents became angry and didn't want to let black children into their schools. There was trouble in Little Rock, Arkansas, over this. President Eisenhower had to send federal troops to make sure the black children got to school safely.

Eisenhower suffered a heart attack. Later he needed an operation for an intestinal illness. He bounced back from these serious illnesses and went on being president, serving from 1953 to 1961. He was still a much-loved president when he retired to writing books and playing golf until his death in 1969.

Recalling the Facts

Write **True** or **False** after each of the following statements. Then exchange papers with a partner to check your answers.

1. Young Eisenhower had a very bad temper. _____

2. Eisenhower was Supreme Commander during World War II. _____

3. Eisenhower ran for president as a Democrat. _____

4. Eisenhower refused to send federal troops to Little Rock to help black children arrive safely in school. _____

5. Eisenhower was an unpopular president. _____

Individual Activities

THE PRICE OF WEAPONS: A POSTER

Eisenhower said, "Every gun that is made, every warship launched, every rocket fired, signifies, in the final sense, a theft from those who hunger and are not fed, those who are cold and are not clothed." Write this on a poster and choose a photograph or drawing that fits the idea.

JONAS SALK: HERO

Research Jonas Salk, who became a true American hero during Eisenhower's term. Find out what he did, and write an article about him or make a poster honoring his achievement.

A LETTER FROM LITTLE ROCK

In 1954, during Eisenhower's presidency, the Supreme Court declared school segregation to be illegal. Imagine you are an African-American student entering Central High in Little Rock in 1954. Write a letter to a friend across town telling how you feel about going to an all-white school where some parents may be angry at you.

JOHN F. KENNEDY

©1967 by Dover Publications, Inc.

Brothers Joe and Jack Kennedy were three years apart in age. Joe was the older son; he was dark haired, strong, and good in sports. Younger Jack, with reddish-brown hair and blue-gray eyes, was always sick and often having accidents. Joe was smart in school, but Jack was only a fair student.

Young Jack was a sickly child with a narrow face. His ears stuck out; some people said he looked like an elf. Once, during a family blueberry hunt, Jack got into trouble again. While his brothers and sisters were collecting berries in pails, Jack sat on an anthill. He yelled and waved his

arms as ants swarmed all over him. Jack was unlucky again!

As Jack grew older, he tried to be like his older brother Joe. But he was never as good at football or anything else. Joe had been a fine student at Choate prep school. He was popular and at the head of his class. Then it was time for Jack to go to Choate. He hated having to go to Choate and once again try to live up to his brother's success.

So when Jack got to Choate, he didn't study much. He played pranks like tossing oranges out the window and stuffing pillows into the rooms. He belonged to a group of mischief makers called the "Muckers Club." Jack's father was called to the school, where he heard Jack described as "not a wicked kid, but a nuisance." Jack's father had a long talk with his son. After that, Jack settled down and did well at Choate—but he never liked it there.

Born in Brookline, Massachusetts, in 1917, John F. Kennedy grew up to become a lieutenant in the Navy during World War II. His torpedo boat, PT 109, was struck by a Japanese destroyer and cut in two. Two sailors were lost and others, including Kennedy, were wounded. One man was seriously burned. Commander Kennedy ordered all the men to swim for an island three miles away. Those sailors too badly wounded to swim hung on to a board and pushed. Kennedy himself pulled the burned sailor along with him. All the men made it safely to the island, and Kennedy was a twenty-six-year-old hero.

At twenty-nine, Kennedy became a congressman. He became ill with a serious spine problem. While recovering, he wrote a book about brave members of Congress called *Profiles in Courage*.

Kennedy was a senator in 1960, when he was chosen to run for president on the Democratic ticket. He was Roman Catholic, and no one from that religion had ever been president. Kennedy was forty-three years old; many said he was too young to be president. But Kennedy won the election in a close vote.

Kennedy called his plan for America the New Frontier. He started the Peace Corps, a program allowing Americans of all ages, but mostly young, to go to poor countries and help out. Kennedy said, "Ask not what your country can do for you. Ask what you can do for your country." Thousands of Americans answered that call and joined the Peace Corps to make the world better.

Early in his presidency, Kennedy supported an attack on Communist-controlled Cuba by Cubans wishing to bring freedom back to their country. It was called the Bay of Pigs invasion. This attack failed, and Communist Fidel Castro remained in power in Cuba. Castro then asked Russia for missiles that he might use against the United States. (Cuba is just ninety miles from the United States.) When Russia gave Cuba the missiles, Kennedy demanded they be removed. For a while it looked as though World War III might break out. But finally Russia took the missiles away, and everybody was thankful.

Kennedy's wife, Jacqueline Bouvier Kennedy, was a talented young woman who could speak French, Spanish, and Italian and paint lovely watercolors. Their small daughter, Caroline, and their son, John Kennedy, Jr., won the hearts of the American people. The vigorous young president and his wife and children seemed to bring exciting new life to the White House.

On November 22, 1963, Kennedy took a trip to Dallas, Texas. He was riding in an open car when shots rang out. The president was fatally wounded. He was the first president assassinated in sixty-two years. A man named Lee Harvey Oswald was arrested and accused of shooting Kennedy from a warehouse window. As Oswald was being led to jail, he was shot and killed by another man who said he loved the president and wanted to get revenge.

After days of national sorrow, Kennedy was buried at Arlington Cemetery. The promising young president had served from 1961 to 1963.

Recalling the Facts

Match each numbered description with a word or phrase below. Write the correct answer in the blank. Then exchange papers with a partner to check your answers.

Lee Harvey Oswald   Choate   Cuba   World War II   Peace Corps

1. Jack Kennedy's prep school

   _____

2. The war in which Kennedy became a hero

   _____

3. Kennedy's plan to send Americans to help poor nations

   _____

4. The man who was accused of shooting Kennedy

   _____

5. Where the Bay of Pigs invasion took place

   _____

Individual Activities

A CONSPIRACY?

Many Americans were never sure that Lee Harvey Oswald acted alone in killing Kennedy. He never had a trial because he was killed. Ask relatives and friends who remember the events of November 22, 1963, if they believed Oswald acted alone. Make a report of their responses.

ASK NOT: A CHALLENGE

If someone said to you personally, "Ask not what your country can do for you. Ask what you can do for your country," what would you say? Write a few sentences telling what you could do for your country.

KENNEDY FAMILY: RESEARCH

In books about the Kennedy family, find out what happened to Joe, Jack's promising older brother. Also find out what happened to Robert F. Kennedy, Jack's younger brother. This American family was wealthy and fortunate, but also struck by great tragedy. Design a monument for Joe or Robert Kennedy based on his life. Draw a picture of it or describe it. Or, photocopy a photograph of either brother and write a brief obituary for him.

LYNDON B. JOHNSON

©1967 by Dover Publications, Inc.

As a boy on a farm near Stonewall, Texas, Lyndon Johnson rode his pony to school. He had a paper route and he earned money shining shoes, but what he enjoyed most was his father's political life. During his father's political campaigns, father and son would ride in a model T from farm to farm, stopping at every door. Lyndon's father was running for the state legislature, and he talked to every family. Most of the time they would ask Lyndon and his father in, offering big crusts of homemade bread and jars of home-canned jelly. In summer the friendly Texans served ice cream, and in winter, hot tea.

Lyndon also loved going to the state legislature once his father was elected. He would sit there and glow with pride when his father got up to make a speech. The political life looked truly wonderful to the boy.

Lyndon was a restless student and a bit of a troublemaker. He was always being punished with extra chores like cleaning the blackboard and bringing in the fire-wood.

Along with his father, Lyndon's grandfather was also a hero in the boy's life. Lyndon's grandfather could tell endless stories about stampedes and cattle drives. After each tale he'd reach into his big roll-top desk and produce a candy or a giant red apple for Lyndon.

A difficult moment came in young Lyndon's life when he delayed becoming a hunter. His disappointed father prodded him into shooting his first rabbit; afterward Lyndon felt sick and sad. He never forgot the bad feeling that first kill gave him.

Born in Stonewall, Texas, in 1908, Lyndon Johnson finished high school and decided he didn't want to go to college. He hitched rides in cars all the way to California and took any job he could get. He washed dishes and waited on tables. He ran elevators and did hard labor with a road-building crew. Life was tougher than Lyndon had expected it would be. Homesick and disappointed, he returned to Texas and went to teachers' college.

Lyndon became a public school teacher, but memories of his father's political career quickly led him from the classroom. He became a congressman, and then, when World War II came, he was a Navy Commander. After the war, Johnson became a U.S. senator. For many years he was a powerful leader in the Senate. He was known as a man who could get things done. In 1960 he ran for vice president on the ticket with John Kennedy.

When Kennedy was shot in Dallas, Johnson was also there. As the body of the dead president lay on the plane, Johnson was sworn in as president on the same plane. Johnson returned to Washington as president. He told the American people he would carry out Kennedy's plans, especially the civil rights programs. One of Johnson's favorite sayings was "Let us reason together." He believed you could accomplish anything by talking about it and making compromises.

Johnson's own program was called the Great Society. He declared war on poverty and put in programs to help poor people have a better life. For example, he started Head Start, a preschool program for poor children. Johnson also started Medicare, government health care for retired Americans. Johnson signed the Civil Rights Bill that gave African Americans more rights.

Johnson improved life for millions of Americans, but his presidency was damaged by a war in Asia.

When Johnson became president, the United States had several thousand American military personnel in South Vietnam. They were helping the government of South Vietnam fight a Communist revolution sponsored by North Vietnam. It was a small war, but America was not winning it. Johnson sent in thousands of more troops. Soon hundreds—and then thousands—of Americans were being wounded and killed in the war. The military men under Johnson kept promising there was "a light at the end of the tunnel" and the war would soon be won. But the war kept on getting worse. Every night Americans watched on television as grim scenes of wounded and dead Americans were shown.

During the last two years of Johnson's second term, there were huge antiwar marches. Americans who wanted to stay in Vietnam and win the war were called *hawks*. Americans who wanted to pull out were called *doves*. Families were divided; the issue was tearing America apart. Most Americans were just weary, and they wanted the war to end.

Johnson surprised the nation by announcing he would not run for reelection in 1968. He had served from 1963 to 1969. He retired to his ranch in Texas, where he died four years later, in 1973.

Recalling the Facts

Circle the correct ending to each of the following sentences. Then exchange papers with a partner to check your answers.

1. On the subject of poverty, Johnson   (a) cared deeply   (b) was not concerned   (c) knew little   (d) did nothing

2. Johnson was a senator who   (a) accomplished little   (b) argued to the point of anger   (c) could get things done   (d) disliked politics

3. Medicare gave health coverage to   (a) children   (b) government workers   (c) the military   (d) retired people

4. Johnson urged people to   (a) study together   (b) play together   (c) pray together   (d) reason together

5. Johnson's presidency was damaged by   (a) a depression   (b) a civil rights fight   (c) the Vietnam War   (d) his wife

Individual Activities

MEDICARE: A SURVEY

Because of Lyndon Johnson, older Americans are covered by government medical insurance. Ask older members of your family, or older friends, if Medicare works for them. Write a short report and tell the class the results.

WILDFLOWERS: A DREAM

While in the White House, Lady Bird Johnson, President Johnson's wife, did much to beautify America—especially its highways. After leaving the White House, she went to work on a related project—to conserve and promote the country's native plants. Find out what wildflowers are native to your area. Make a poster featuring one. Plant some wildflowers in season.

LETTER TO EDITOR

Lyndon Johnson left the presidency an unhappy and much-criticized man, but he did accomplish great things. Write a letter to an imaginary newspaper editor praising Johnson for one of his successes.

RICHARD M. NIXON

©1967 by Dover Publications, Inc.

Dick Nixon was not popular as a child. He played baseball, but he was small and clumsy. He was too serious for most of his classmates. Even in first grade, he insisted on coming to school in a white shirt, black bow tie, and neat knee pants—even though he was barefoot. His parents couldn't afford to buy him shoes. Dick never wanted to get dirty, so rough play was out of the question.

Because the Nixon family was poor, supper often was just cornmeal. But Hannah Nixon always made sure her children did the right thing. When Dick took a bunch of grapes from a neighbor's vine without asking, his mother made him pay the neighbor back from his precious jar of pennies.

In his teens Dick worked at his parents' grocery store and gas station in Whittier, California. Each morning he got up at 4 A.M. and drove to the vegetable market in downtown Los Angeles to get fresh produce. Then he returned to Whittier and set up the vegetables before going to high school.

At high school the other boys called Dick "gloomy Gus" after a cartoon character who was always grim. At seventeen Dick won a scholarship to Harvard, but he couldn't take it because his older brother was dying of tuberculosis; the family needed Dick at home. So young Nixon went to Whittier College, where the campus newspaper dubbed him Nicky, a name he hated. Said a college acquaintance, "Nixon was not a guy you'd put on a backpack and go fishing with." However, Nixon did become president of the student body at Whittier.

Born in Yorba Linda, California, in 1913, Richard Nixon studied law at Duke University. While there, he moved into a cardboard and tin shed behind the school to save the expense of the dorms. He wanted money to buy his mother a fur coat. Always devoted to his family, Nixon didn't have a warm relationship with strangers.

Nixon was a serious and hardworking student at Duke. He dreamed of being very successful one day. His fellow students were amazed by how hard he worked. One said, "If this fellow keeps it up this way he is going, someday he will be president."

During World War II, Nixon served for four years in the navy. After the war he settled into a law practice until 1947, when he became a congressman. He became well known as someone interested in uncovering Communist spies in the United States. He belonged to the House Un-American Activities Committee. In a famous case, Nixon accused Alger Hiss, a state department official, of passing secret papers to a Communist spy ring. Nixon became famous all over America because of this case. He said "The Hiss case brought me national fame," but he added, "but it left a residue of hatred and hostility toward me."

In 1950 Nixon became a U.S. senator. Two years later, at thirty-nine, he became the youngest vice president in American history. He served under President Eisenhower for eight years. In 1960 Nixon ran for president against John Kennedy. During their debates Kennedy looked young and handsome; Nixon, with his heavy jowls, bushy eyebrows, and perspiring face, looked bad. The television camera was not kind to Nixon.

In 1968, after losing a try to become California governor, Nixon ran again for the presidency. This time, because the Vietnam War had divided the country, Nixon won.

He slowly pulled American troops out of Vietnam and started talking to Russia about cutting back on weapons. Nixon rebuilt the American friendship with China. Nixon made the world safer by promoting peace. He was the first president to set up an agency to take care of the environment.

In 1972 Nixon ran for reelection. Nixon was popular at the time, but he was very suspicious of what strategy the Democrats would use against him. Nixon's followers broke into the Democratic National Party headquarters at the Watergate building in Washington to find out what the Democrats were planning. Nixon tried to cover up the break-in, which soon turned into a big problem. When Nixon discussed the Watergate break-in with his advisors, he taped the conversations. Then he was forced to turn the tapes over to a judge. The tapes proved that Nixon had tried to cover up crimes and had not told the truth. Nixon was threatened with impeachment. He decided to resign the presidency instead. He was the only president ever to be forced to resign. After serving from 1969 to 1974, Nixon flew back to California.

Nixon returned to private life a sad man. But then he made trips around the world to promote world peace. He died in 1994 and was buried near his childhood home.

Recalling the Facts

Circle the best ending to each of the following sentences. Then exchange papers with a partner to check your answers.

1. Young Nixon went to first grade in (a) a cowboy suit (b) blue jeans (c) white shirt and tie (d) a helmet

2. Nixon couldn't attend Harvard because of (a) low grades (b) homesickness (c) a need for him at home (d) his attitude toward study

3. Nixon ran for president in (a) 1960, 1968, 1972 (b) 1972, 1976, 1980 (c) 1980, 1984, 1988 (d) 1984, 1988, 1992

4. Nixon covered up a crime of (a) arson (b) spying (c) breaking in (d) murder

5. Nixon was the first president to (a) run three times (b) serve eight years as vice president (c) belong to a third party (d) resign from office

Individual Activities

PANDA POWER

Nixon rebuilt relations with China. As a goodwill gift, the Chinese government loaned America some giant pandas. Draw a cartoon featuring pandas with the theme of U.S.–China friendship.

NIXON'S CLASSMATES: AN OPINION

Imagine you were a classmate of Richard Nixon in elementary school, high school, and Whittier College. He has asked you to write a reference letter for him. Write such a letter, giving your honest opinion of him as a student.

RISE TO POWER

Richard Nixon rose up very fast to become the youngest vice president ever up to that point. Write a paragraph listing the personal qualities that you think helped Nixon rise so fast.

GERALD R. FORD

©1995 UPI/BETTMANN

Jerry Ford was a popular high school senior. He was first-string center for South High School. Tall, strong, and friendly, Jerry had just made the all-state team. And he'd just bought his very first car—an old model T Ford.

Jerry had saved his own money to buy the car. Having it meant he wouldn't have to ride the bus or walk to school anymore. He was on top of the world.

One cold day after driving his car, Jerry worried that the engine would freeze. He covered the engine with a blanket and then went inside to eat dinner.

"Something burning on the stove?" asked Jerry's father. Jerry's mother went to check in the kitchen. Everything was all right there, but where was that terrible burning smell coming from?

Jerry rushed outside to see his precious car in flames. The blanket Jerry had tenderly placed over the hot engine had caught fire. In a few minutes the car was burned up, even though the fire department came to help.

"Don't worry, son," said Jerry's father. "Remember when I told you to buy insurance for your car? Well now you can collect on it and buy a new car."

Jerry hung his head. He'd forgotten to buy insurance! He was out of a car—and out of money too.

Jerry walked to school or rode the bus for the rest of his senior year, but he kept on playing football.

Born in Omaha, Nebraska, in 1913, Gerald Ford was voted the most popular senior in high school. His reward was a trip to Washington, D.C. It would be his first trip to Washington, but not his last.

Ford served in the navy during World War II. Then he practiced law. Soon he was elected to the House of Representatives from Michigan. Ford was reelected thirteen times. A smiling, warmhearted common man, Ford was well respected by everyone who knew him. He loved his job in Congress and never wanted any other.

But something nobody expected changed his future.

In 1973 the vice president of the United States was Spiro Agnew. He was accused of not reporting honestly on his income tax forms. He was forced to resign the job of vice president in the middle of his term.

President Nixon now needed to find a new vice president. He wanted someone very respected and honest so that Congress would accept him as the new vice president. The likable Gerald Ford seemed perfect, so he was chosen by Nixon and approved by Congress.

Nixon himself was in trouble; he had covered up the Watergate break-in at the Democratic headquarters in Washington. So, in 1974, Nixon resigned the presidency, and Gerald Ford was sworn in as president in August. Ford said, "Our long national nightmare is over." For months the American people had watched as stories of lies and cover-ups flooded television and the press. Now, at last, there would be a new president not under accusation.

Ford brought the remaining American troops home from Vietnam. In a desperate rush to escape the Communists, thousands of Vietnamese fled; many came to America.

Ford was an honest, open, friendly president. After the secretive and quiet Nixon, this was very welcome. It helped people get over the pain of Watergate.

Ford made no big changes from the Nixon years. He continued to build up national defense while searching for peace at the same time. Ford pardoned former President Nixon, who still faced problems for what he did during the Watergate period. Ford did this to spare America the shame of having a former president on trial. He also wanted to spare the Nixon family more sadness and pain. Ford, who was a generous man, did this out of kindness, but many Americans did not like the decision. They wanted to punish Nixon for whatever crimes he may have committed while covering up the break-in. They believed that not even the president should be able to get away with anything.

When many Americans became jobless during Ford's presidency, he urged everybody to go out and buy something to get the economy moving again. It didn't work, and the American economy remained slow. When Ford ran for president in 1976, he was defeated. Some people blamed the fact that he had pardoned Nixon for his loss.

Ford had served from 1974 to 1977. He returned to private life, often playing golf with his friends. He had been just the person America needed at a difficult time.

Recalling the Facts

Write **True** or **False** after each of the following statements. Then exchange papers with a partner to check your answers.

1. As a teenager, Ford was a good baseball player.   _____

2. Ford was elected to Congress thirteen times.   _____

3. Ford always wanted to be president.   _____

4. Ford refused to pardon former President Nixon.   _____

5. Ford said, "Our long national nightmare is over."   _____

Individual Activities

FOOTBALL: A TRAINING GROUND?

Gerald Ford was a fine football player. Do you think there were things he learned playing football that helped him in politics and in the presidency? List three skills a person might learn on the football field that would help a political leader.

BUY AMERICAN

President Ford urged all Americans to buy some American products so more people would have jobs in this country. Design a poster showing some American-made products. Write a catchy slogan urging consumers to buy American.

YOUNG JERRY FORD: A DIARY ENTRY

Imagine you are young Ford who has just found his burned-up automobile. You have a diary; tonight you will write about this minor tragedy. Write the events down as Ford may have.

JIMMY CARTER

©1995 UPI/BETTMANN

When Jimmy Carter was a boy, African-American and white children lived lives apart from each other. They went to separate schools, even if they lived across the street from each other. Usually the two groups of children did not play together. This was not the case with young Jimmy. He always played with the black children who lived in the black community of Archery. Jimmy and his black companions built a tree house together, fished, hunted, and rode their horses and mules over the red Georgia clay. Though he was a southern boy, Jimmy grew up looking at everybody as equal.

Jimmy lived on a peanut farm in Plains, Georgia, in the 1920's and 1930's. A lot of people were out of work because America was in a depression. Jimmy wanted to do his part to help his family get along, so he went into the peanut business on his own.

Every morning at dawn, barefoot and shirtless in the warm Georgia summer, Jimmy pulled a wagon out to the peanut fields. He pulled the peanuts from the ground, shook the dirt off, then piled them in a wagon. He picked the peanuts from the vines and soaked the peanuts overnight. Then Jimmy built an outdoor fire and boiled the peanuts he'd picked the day before in a black pot. He carefully measured out half a pound of peanuts for each of twenty bags. After breakfast the boy took the bags to town and sold them at five cents each. He made a dollar a day at a time when many people were making less. As he grew older, Jimmy helped raise cotton, corn, watermelons, potatoes—and, of course, more peanuts.

Born in 1924 in Plains, Georgia, Jimmy Carter went to school at the United States Naval Academy during World War II. After the war, he served on a submarine. Then he came home to be a peanut farmer.

In the 1960's, Carter was elected to the state legislature. Later he became governor of Georgia. He said he wanted to help people. He had learned a lot from his mother, Lillian Carter. A sixty-eight-year-old widow, she went to India as a Peace Corps volunteer to care for the sick.

Carter was not well known in 1976 when he ran for president as a Democrat, but the American people liked him. He had a wide grin and down-to-earth ways. He seemed like an ordinary, honest man at a time when many people were tired of politicians.

When Carter became president, he walked to the White House with his wife and young daughter, Amy. Amy was the first child in the White House since the Kennedy children. In keeping with their principles, Carter and his wife Roselyn sent Amy to public school in Washington.

Carter brought the leaders of Israel and Egypt together to sign a peace treaty. This was an important success, for these two countries had long been at war.

Two years after Carter became president, a serious problem came up in distant Iran. For a long time Iran had been ruled by the Shah. He had been a good friend of the United States, but many in Iran hated him. During a revolution in Iran, the Shah was thrown out of the country. When the Shah became very ill with cancer, he asked to come to the United States for treatment. The new government in Iran warned that there would be trouble if this man they hated were allowed into the United States. Carter felt sorry for the Shah and allowed him in for treatment. A large group of young Iranians then attacked the United States Embassy in Iran. They took sixty

Americans who worked there prisoner. They paraded the blindfolded American captives around the streets and mocked them. The Iranians burned American flags. This was seen nightly on American television. Angry and shamed, the American people demanded that President Carter do something about it.

Carter sent a rescue mission to get the hostages out, but it failed. He feared taking more drastic action, because the Iranians threatened to kill the American hostages. So the Americans remained hostages; many people blamed Carter.

At this time many Americans were out of work, and prices were soaring. Carter was also blamed for these problems. In 1980, when he ran for reelection, he lost. After serving from 1977 to 1981, Carter returned to private life. Unlike most former presidents who spend their time enjoying life and writing books, Carter and his wife, Roselyn, and even daughter Amy went to work building houses for poor Americans. They really hammered and sawed with other craftspeople. This made Carter one of America's most respected former presidents.

In recent years, Carter has traveled around the world to trouble spots such as Haiti and the countries that were formerly Yugoslavia. He has helped arrange truces in civil wars, and he has been a powerful voice for compromise and peace. He has been so successful that he has earned the respect of people all over the world.

Recalling the Facts

Match each numbered description with one of the words or phrases below. Write the answer in the blank. Then exchange papers with a partner to check your answers.

Amy Carter   Shah   peanuts   Lillian Carter   Egypt

1. Young Carter sold bags of these to make money.   _____

2. This Peace Corps volunteer inspired Carter.   _____

3. The first child in the White House since the Kennedy years.   _____

4. The man who came to the U.S. for cancer treatment.   _____

5. Carter made peace between leaders of Israel and this country.   _____

Individual Activities

MISERY INDEX

During Carter's term, people heard a lot about the "misery index." The misery index is the percentage of Americans unemployed added to interest rates being charged. In 1980 the unemployment rate was 7%; the interest rate was about 13%. So the misery index was 20%—very high. Look in an almanac or other source to find the present unemployment and interest rates. What is the misery index now?

LILLIAN CARTER

Research the life of Carter's mother, especially her years in the Peace Corps. Write a fitting obituary for this remarkable woman.

CARTER WAS A HUMBLE PRESIDENT: A CARTOON

Find a cartoon from the years 1978 to 1980 showing Carter as a humble man (like walking to his swearing-in). Or draw such a cartoon using stick figures if you wish.

RONALD REAGAN

©1995 UPI/BETTMANN

Fifteen-year-old Ronald "Dutch" Reagan sat up on the lifeguard station. He kept staring at the dangerous Rock River in Lowell Park. When there was a lot of rain, the river rushed through the park. Its powerful currents had already taken several lives.

Previously, in the spring of 1926, the people of Dixon, Illinois, were about to close Lowell Park's only outdoor swimming area. Then a tall, thin boy with thick glasses asked for the job of lifeguard. Dutch Reagan got the job. He immediately began giving swimming lessons to the younger children who came by. One of them was nine-year-old Bill Thompson. One day while Bill sat on a log, he heard a man

scream in the water. He was drowning in the fast current. Bill shouted, "Get him, Dutch!" Dutch had already sprung into action.

Dutch threw down his glasses and dove right into Rock River. He swam through the rough water like a torpedo, grabbed the drowning man, and pulled him to shore. Then Dutch breathed into the man's mouth until he could breathe normally on his own again. Finally Dutch put his glasses back on and carved a notch in the log near the river.

Every time Dutch saved somebody's life, he carved a notch in the log. At the end of seven summers spent as lifeguard in Lowell Park, seventy-seven notches were in the log. Not one swimmer had drowned on Dutch's watch.

Born in Tampico, Illinois, in 1911, Ronald Reagan worked for Ringling Brothers Circus dragging circus wagons into the mud so they wouldn't roll away. At Eureka College he was a good athlete and a popular boy who liked acting.

After college, Reagan drove to Station WOC in Davenport, Iowa, and tried for a job as sports reporter. He got the job, and became the sports voice of the Midwest until he was twenty-six. Then Reagan headed for Hollywood to try his luck in the movies. He was signed by Warner Brothers, and he made fifty-four movies during his career. Reagan was not a great actor; many of his movies were small and unimportant.

The movie *Kings Row*, however, was a fine picture, and Reagan's work was praised.

Reagan became active in the Screen Actors Guild, the actors union. He then got interested in Republican politics. A fine speaker with a gift for talking to people and winning them over, Reagan was perfect for television. In 1964 Reagan made a speech for the Republican candidate Barry Goldwater. Goldwater lost, but it was a great speech. People remembered Reagan.

In 1966 Reagan ran for governor of California. The Democrat he ran against made fun of Reagan's background as an actor. Once Reagan had made a movie called *Bedtime for Bonzo*, in which he played with a monkey. To make Reagan appear foolish, Reagan's opponent put out ads showing Reagan and the monkey. But Reagan won the election and became governor of California.

In 1980 Reagan ran for president. He asked the American people this question: Are you better or worse off now than when Carter was elected four years ago? Reagan won a big victory. On the day he took office, Iran released the sixty American hostages they had seized during Carter's presidency.

As president, Reagan cut taxes and cut government spending on some things. But he continued to spend a lot on national defense. He won victories in Congress by going directly to the people on television. He was called the "great communicator" because he could reach the people.

After being president just three months, Reagan was shot by a mentally ill man. The man wanted to do something to get the attention of an actress he had a crush on. The bullet struck close to Reagan's heart, but surgeons did a good job; soon he was on the road to recovery. Reagan joked with the doctors as he was carried on a stretcher, which made him even more popular with the people. The smiling president seemed indestructible.

Reagan made important deals with Russia. He also chose the first woman ever to serve on the Supreme Court—Sandra Day O'Connor. But during his two terms, the national debt—money owed by the United States—soared. After serving from 1981 to 1989, Reagan returned to private life. His eight years saw a good economy, low prices, and peace. He was still popular. He went to his beloved ranch in California to ride horses and write books.

Recalling the Facts

Following is a list of events that occurred during Ronald Reagan's life. The events are out of order. In the blanks before the sentences, number the events in the correct order. Exchange papers with a partner to check your answers.

(a) _____ Reagan became an actor at Warner Brothers.

(b) _____ Reagan was elected president.

(c) _____ Reagan saved a man from drowning.

(d) _____ Reagan appointed the first woman to serve on the Supreme Court, Sandra Day O'Connor.

(e) _____ Reagan became governor of California.

Individual Activities

JUST SAY NO: A POSTER

Nancy Reagan, the president's wife, worked hard on stopping drug abuse. Her campaign was called "Just say no" to drugs. Make a poster warning against drugs, including alcohol and tobacco.

PREJUDICE AGAINST THE OLD: A SLOGAN

Some people said that Reagan, at sixty-eight and then at seventy-two, was too old to be president. He always made a joke about his age. Once he told his opponent who was in his fifties, "If you overlook my old age, I'll overlook your youth." Write a slogan that makes the point that you are never too old to accomplish things. Write it on a poster, and attach a photo of an active older American.

REAGAN'S COWBOY IMAGE

Reagan, who played in some cowboy movies, was often pictured on his horse. What is your opinion of a cowboy? Do you think having a "cowboy image" helped Reagan? Answer in a paragraph.

GEORGE BUSH

Teenage George Bush joined the navy during World War II. Before long he was a lieutenant, junior grade, piloting his Avenger plane. One day he made dive-bomb attacks on a Japanese-held island in the Pacific Ocean. Bush's plane was hit. His engine on fire, Bush shouted to his crew the command "Hit the silk." It meant they should bail out, as he was doing.

The wind tore at Bush's parachute as he plunged over the side of the plane. He banged his head and cut his forehead. Air driven backwards threw him into the tail of the plane. The parachute got caught and ripped.

For the last twenty feet, Bush went straight down into the water. He quickly jerked the pins on his flight suit to get out of the heavy clothing. He removed his shoes and treaded water before swimming to the raft that had also dropped from the plane.

Bush found that the raft had lost its paddles. There was no way to move the raft except by hand-paddling. The fresh-water container was smashed. Bush was sick from swallowing sea water, and his arm was burned from jellyfish stings.

Bush paddled by hand through the choppy green water. He feared the Japanese would find him before the Americans rescued him. But less than two hours later, he saw the fin of a United States submarine. Soon American sailors scrambled around the raft. The young pilot was pulled to safety. George Bush was saved; he was suddenly a hero.

Born in Milton, Massachusetts, in 1924, George Bush won the Distinguished Flying Cross as a pilot before he was twenty-one. As a small boy in a wealthy family, Bush watched his parents visit with famous world leaders.

After Yale University, Bush entered the oil business in Texas. He became a wealthy man himself, but he was interested in politics. He was elected to the House of Representatives.

Beyond the Cherry Tree: Stories of the Presidents

Bush was appointed to many important government jobs. He worked at the United Nations and at the Central Intelligence Agency. In 1980 he was chosen to run as vice president with Ronald Reagan.

For eight years Bush was a faithful vice president to President Reagan. He never disagreed publicly with the popular president. In 1988 it was Bush's turn to run for president, and he was easily elected.

When Bush became president, the United States economy was running well. America was at peace. Bush did not promise to do many new things, because it seemed everything was fine as it was.

Bush had a problem when there was an uprising in Panama. He sent American troops there to capture the president of Panama and to arrest him on drug charges. This was called Operation Just Cause. It was called a big success, because the new government that came to Panama was more democratic.

Bush continued to spend a lot of money on national defense. Because Reagan and now Bush did this, the national debt went up even more. When a country spends more money than it takes in, it has to borrow money. The national debt tells us how much money we owe.

Bush also continued to build friendships with Russia and China. During Bush's term in office, an amazing thing happened in the world: Russian Communism fell apart. The countries in Eastern Europe that had been under Russian control for so long were now free. This put an end to the Cold War that had been a fact of life for almost forty years.

In 1991 Iraq, under its leader Saddam Hussein, attacked and took over the small oil-rich country of Kuwait. Kuwait was a friend of the United States. Bush ordered Iraqis out of Kuwait, but they wouldn't leave. Saddam Hussein said that Kuwait was now part of Iraq. Bush set up Operation Desert Storm and sent thousands of American troops to drive Iraq from Kuwait. The war was very brief and Kuwait was freed. Bush's popularity rose as huge parades were held celebrating the returning heroes of Desert Storm. They had a big victory; America was in a happy mood. There were yellow ribbons and American flags flying everywhere.

Everybody expected Bush would be easily reelected in 1992, but bad economic times struck. Many people were jobless. Bush kept on saying that nothing was wrong and he didn't have to do anything. By the time Bush saw the truth, it was too late. He lost the election after serving from 1989 to 1993. He returned to private life, to enjoy his large family and his hobbies of sailing and fishing.

Recalling the Facts

Match the descriptions with the word or words listed below them. Write the letter of the correct answer in the blank. Then exchange papers with a partner to check your answers.

Panama   pilot   China   Kuwait   American economy

1. What Bush was as a teenager   _____

2. Where Operation Just Cause took place   _____

3. Bush continued better relations with this country and Russia.   _____

4. Where Operation Desert Storm took place   _____

5. This cost Bush the election in 1992.   _____

Individual Activities

LIEUTENANT BUSH: A NEWS STORY

Imagine you were a news reporter at the time of young Bush's heroism. Write an account of what happened, including the exciting details. Look at news items in the paper to see how news stories are written.

KUWAIT TODAY

President Bush's actions saved Kuwait. Do some research on Kuwait today. What is happening there? Check magazine and newspaper articles about Kuwait and write a short report.

FOREIGN OR DOMESTIC? A SURVEY

President Bush was very good at solving problems with foreign countries. He was not as good at solving domestic problems, such as the economic troubles that caused many Americans to lose their jobs. Using the following two questions, survey adults and people your age. Then give the results to the class.

Do you think it's more important for a president to be good at solving foreign problems or domestic problems?

What is your most important issue in voting for a president?

BILL CLINTON

© 1995 UPI/BETTMANN

Bill Clinton turned seventeen in the summer of 1963. He had been at a camp called Boys State, where students learned all about politics. Bill was elected to Boys Nation, which meant he could go to Washington to visit politicians and historic sites.

On a warm July day, Bill and the other boys headed for the White House. Bill's mind went back to a day in 1956. He had been watching the Democratic national convention on television. Bill loved it. He remembered seeing a handsome young senator named John F. Kennedy at that convention.

Now the smiling young Senator Kennedy was president of the United States, and Bill was about to meet him. Bill trembled with excitement as President Kennedy strode out into the Rose Garden. Moments later the teenager from Hope, Arkansas, Bill Clinton, was shaking hands with the man he'd long admired, President Kennedy. It was a turning point in Bill's heart and mind. He hadn't known what he wanted to be before, but now he knew. He would be a politician.

Bill's mother never forgot the light in her son's eyes when he returned from Washington. Bill was "holding this picture of himself with Jack Kennedy," Bill's mother said, "I knew right then that politics was the answer for him."

Born in Hope, Arkansas, in 1946, Bill Clinton was elected attorney general of Arkansas when he was twenty-nine. At thirty-two he became governor of Arkansas, the state's youngest governor ever. Clinton served for several terms as governor. Then, in 1992, he decided to run for president.

Clinton promised he would help "grow" America by making new jobs. This was a welcome promise, because many Americans were out of work. Big companies were cutting down on the number of people they employed. Thousands were losing their jobs in the defense industry, because the Cold War between the free world and the Communist world seemed to be over.

Clinton also promised to provide health care for all Americans. In the years between 1970 and 1990, the cost of medical care had gone up greatly. So the prices people had to pay for medical insurance had increased too. For example, one person had to pay $11 a month for medical insurance in 1970, and $84 a month in 1990.

The political campaign between Bush and Clinton was very rough. Clinton was attacked as a person who did not have character. Some blamed him for not serving in the military during the Vietnam War. Also, Clinton had taken part in protests against the Vietnam War as a young man. Clinton's wife, Hillary Rodham Clinton, was an attorney in Arkansas and was a strong-minded woman. Some people did not feel comfortable with a woman who for many years made more money than her husband.

Clinton was not popular when the campaign began, and everybody expected Bush would win. But little by little Clinton won the favor of more Americans. He won the election by winning thirty-one states.

Immediately after becoming president, Clinton raised the taxes on Americans who are considered rich. He put Hillary Rodham Clinton in charge of writing the new health program. After many months of work, a health plan was announced, but it was very complicated. Most people didn't understand it and were afraid of it. Clinton's health plan began a very slow path through Congress.

In 1994 the Whitewater problem came up. Back in 1989 a bank in Arkansas had gone out of business. Some said that millions from this bank went to help a real estate company called Whitewater. Clinton was a partner in the Whitewater company.

Clinton wanted to work on problems in America, but world problems kept coming up. The world feared that North Korea was going to make nuclear bombs. Clinton worked out an agreement that allowed inspections in North Korea. Clinton sent American troops to Haiti to put the elected president, Jean-Bertrand Aristide, back in office after a military revolution had forced him out. Then, when it looked as if Iraq could attack Kuwait again, Clinton sent troops there to prevent an invasion.

Like all presidents, Clinton soon found out that it was easier to *run* for president than to *be* president.

Recalling the Facts

Circle the best ending to each of the following sentences. Then exchange papers with a partner to check your answers.

1. Young Clinton really admired   (a) Jimmy Carter   (b) John Kennedy
   (c) Dwight Eisenhower   (d) Franklin Roosevelt

2. As a teenager Clinton went to   (a) Washington   (b) New York   (c) Europe   (d) China

3. At thirty-two Clinton was elected   (a) senator   (b) congressman   (c) governor
   (d) judge

4. The big issue in the 1992 election was   (a) Communism   (b) trade policies
   (c) pollution   (d) jobs

5. Clinton had a problem with a real estate company called   (a) Whitewater
   (b) Watergate   (c) Badwater   (d) Waterworks

Individual Activities

MAN FROM HOPE

Do you think the American people got what they hoped for from the "man from Hope"? Give your opinion, commenting on what was hoped for and what happened.

CHELSEA CLINTON: A LETTER

Chelsea Clinton, Bill Clinton's daughter, became the victim of unkind remarks about her appearance after her father became president. Imagine that you are Chelsea Clinton. Write a letter to the press asking to be allowed to be a normal teenager out of the limelight.

CARTOONS

Find a contemporary political cartoon about the current president. What is the message of the cartoon you chose? If the cartoon ridicules the president, how could you change the cartoon to reverse the message?

TEACHER'S GUIDE

George Washington (page 1)

Answer key: 1. adventure   2. against   3. lived   4. led   5. Mister

CLASS DISCUSSION

1. What qualities do you think are important in a military leader? Did Washington have those qualities? What qualities, if any, did he lack that might have made him a better commander?

2. Washington was described as "first in war, first in peace, and first in the hearts of his countrymen." He was greatly praised after his death, but criticized often during his life. What kinds of things do you think Americans of his time could have criticized in Washington?

GROUP ACTIVITIES

Paintings of George Washington

Have students research some of the famous paintings of George Washington. In their history text, encyclopedias, or biographies of Washington, have them find the answers to questions such as: Did Washington actually pose for the portrait? Did the artist use another artist's painting as the model for his? If so, why? Do the portraits of Washington have anything in common, such as a similar pose? Have students report to the class about their conclusions and what insights they may have gained.

The American Flag

Have students work in teams to prepare a bulletin-board display of the history of the American flag. Assign each team one of the following flags:

the Betsy Ross flag (1777)
the Star-Spangled Banner (1795)
the revised flag (1818)
the 36-star flag (1865–1867)
the 48-star flag (1917–1959)
the 49-star flag (1959–1960)
the 50-star flag (present)

Have members of each team write a paragraph about the history of their assigned flag and either photocopy or make a drawing of the flag. Mount the flags and explanations on a bulletin board along with some of the designs students may have created for "The Betsy Ross Flag and Your Flag" activity on page 3. Discuss the flags and the symbols that are used.

Battlefields of the Revolution

Have students look through a historic atlas and/or U.S. history text and list the major battles of the American Revolution. Divide the class into teams. Assign one site to each team; have team members research what happened there and what the site is like today. Have teams present their findings to the class.

John Adams (page 4)

Answer key: 1. c   2. b   3. b   4. c   5. d

CLASS DISCUSSION

1. John Adams believed that when a lot of Americans complain about the government, the nation is weakened. Is this true? Is there a difference between destructive criticism and arguing for changes to resolve a situation? Ask students to cite examples of constructive criticism.

2. Adams thought that gentlemen—men who owned property and had good educations—could vote more wisely than ordinary people who rented their houses and had little education. Do you think that having a good education improves your voting choices? Does owning property?

GROUP ACTIVITIES

Hunting Debate

One of young John Adams's favorite activities was hunting. Refer to instructions for conducting debates on page *vii*. Then ask students to debate whether or not hunting is beneficial to individuals, society, and wildlife.

The Perfect Teacher

Adams blamed his teacher for the fact that he didn't like school. Actually, Adams was more interested in other things than schoolwork. Still, teachers do make a difference. Assign teams of three or four students to describe a perfect teacher, including time spent on various subjects, amount of homework, what field trips are beneficial, etc. Stress that teachers shouldn't offer only what is fun and easy, but also what will help students learn.

News Events from 1797 to 1801

Have students look up and list some of the major events that took place in the United States and the world while Adams served as president. Examples are the federal government moving from Philadelphia to Washington, French raids on U.S. shipping, launching of U.S. frigates *United States, Constellation,* and *Constitution* (Old Ironsides), Napoleon Bonaparte becoming dictator in France (1799), and revolutionary uprisings in Europe. Have students rank the events in order of their importance to the United States. Or have them prepare a bulletin-board display featuring scenes from the events, which they have drawn or photocopied from books.

Thomas Jefferson (page 7)

Answer key: 1. a   2. d   3. b   4. a   5. d

CLASS DISCUSSION

1. What experiences do you think shaped Jefferson's character the most? He was without a father as a young teenager. He spent many hours alone in the wilderness and he read numerous books. He had a long period of contact with Indian people, including their leaders. What might he have gained from each experience?

2. Today's laws state that a person must be at least thirty-five to be president. Do you favor lowering the age, and, if so, to what age? Jefferson was thirty-three years old when he wrote the Declaration of Independence. Do you think people were more mature in Jefferson's time than they are now. If so, why would that be?

GROUP ACTIVITIES

Weather Report Project

Jefferson kept a daily weather report. For students who share his keen interest in science, ask them each to choose a city in the United States and keep a daily record of high and low temperatures and rainfall (or snowfall) in that city. One student might also keep a record of weather conditions in the community where the classroom is located. At the end of a month, have those students each make a poster featuring the weather in his or her city, including highest and lowest temperatures, day of highest precipitation, and other information. Display the posters and have students compare and discuss their findings.

Trek of Lewis and Clark

Assign student teams to find books about the Lewis and Clark expedition in the library. Have the teams photocopy sketches of some of the animals drawn in the Lewis and Clark journal and then draw or photocopy those animals as they actually look. Neither Lewis nor Clark was an artist. Point out that Lewis and Clark also brought back actual specimens of creatures—such as mountain quail and horned toads. These were then painted by the great artist Charles Willson Peale. Students might photocopy Peale's paintings in order to compare them with the sketches in the Lewis and Clark journal.

Fossils

Jefferson enjoyed collecting fossils. Have each member of the class press a leaf or small object—such as a small tool, nail, or bottle key—into a square of clay, leaving an impression. Other class members will then try to guess what kind of plant or object left the mark. Point out to students that impressions left in the earth are often all we have from earlier civilizations.

James Madison (page 10)

Answer key: 1. True   2. False   3. False   4. False   5. False

CLASS DISCUSSION

1. What can be learned from the challenge Madison faced as a boy? How did he probably think of himself? Do you think he believed he would have a bright future? Looking at what he did in his adult life, what can young people today learn from Madison's life and his ability to overcome problems?

2. Madison left America a more respected nation after his presidency. What changes did he make that caused other nations to take America more seriously? Do you think America is respected by most other nations today? If so, why? If not, why not?

GROUP ACTIVITIES

Bill of Rights

Post a copy of the Bill of Rights in the classroom. Have students form groups to research the history and meaning of each of the ten amendments. Then organize the class into seven groups (amendments 3–4, 6–7, 9–10 work well together) to present their amendment(s) by oral reports or by visual presentations (large photo collages, drawings, or video illustrating freedom being exercised).

The National Anthem

"The Star-Spangled Banner" was written during Madison's term. Play a recording of it in class. Then play other patriotic songs like "My Country 'Tis of Thee," "America the Beautiful," "God Bless America," or others students might suggest. Have students vote on whether or not the present national anthem should be replaced, and if so, by what.

Voices of Authority

President Madison's weak voice did not harm his political future, because the average American of his time never heard him speak. Still, Madison feared his voice would be a detriment. Play a tape of the current president's voice. Ask the students to discuss its weak and strong points. Have student volunteers make brief political speeches (either original or a short reading of a politician's speech). Tape their speeches and play them for the class. Ask which student, based on voice alone, would make the likeliest politician.

James Monroe (page 13)

Answer key: 1. Washington   2. Jefferson   3. good feelings   4. Monroe Doctrine   5. hopeful

CLASS DISCUSSION

1. The basic idea behind the Monroe Doctrine was to tell the nations of Europe that they had no right to interfere in the countries of South America. The United States believed the whole Western Hemisphere to be in its sphere of influence—a special area under U.S. protection and guidance. Did the United States have the right to do this? Why or why not?

2. During Monroe's term, Americans generally felt good about their country. The future looked very bright to most people (excepting, of course, those African Americans held in slavery). Do you think most people feel good about America today? What are the best and worst things about America today?

GROUP ACTIVITIES

Saved from the Guillotine: One-Act Play

Before Monroe became president, he was a diplomat in Paris. Elizabeth Kortright Monroe, his wife, played an important role in saving the life of Madame Lafayette, wife of the Marquis de Lafayette, a friend of America during the Revolution. Tell students to be prepared to perform in a one-act play based on these events:

During the French Revolution, many upper-class or wealthy French persons were put on trial and executed by the guillotine, a big knifelike device. Mrs. Monroe rode in her carriage to the prison where Madame Lafayette was awaiting execution. Mrs. Monroe demanded to see the prisoner. This showed that America would be unhappy if Madame Lafayette were executed. Because Mrs. Monroe spoke on her behalf, Madame Lafayette was released from prison.

Select students to play Mrs. Monroe pleading for the life of Madame Lafayette, Madame Lafayette, and prison guards. Students may wish to read about the French Revolution and then improvise the dialogue. For example, Mrs. Monroe might say, "The American people love the Lafayettes and don't want them harmed."

Monroe Doctrine Legacy

Organize the class into teams to research current conditions in the following South American countries. They were all protected from European intervention by the Monroe Doctrine.

Argentina
Colombia
Venezuela
Brazil
Peru

Teams should then report their findings to the class.

Missouri Compromise

The Missouri Compromise was agreed upon during Monroe's term. Give students copies of the outline map of the United States on page *ix*. Have students draw in and label the states and territories that were free after the Missouri Compromise and those that had slavery. Then have them refer to a historical atlas and draw in Mason and Dixon's line, which formed the southern boundary of Pennsylvania, or 36° 30' north latitude. Students might also make a large map, with the same information, to be posted in the classroom.

John Quincy Adams *(page 16)*

Answer key: 1. True   2. True   3. True   4. False   5. True

CLASS DISCUSSION

1. John Quincy Adams was the son of a president. No child of a president has become president since. Do you think being a president's son made him a better president?

What experiences as a president's son probably helped the most? Why do you think children of presidents rarely even try to become president themselves?

2. Some elected officials vote according to how the people want them to vote. Others, like Adams, always vote according to their own beliefs, even if the voters do not agree. Should an elected official vote according to the wishes of the voters, or according to personal beliefs and principles?

GROUP ACTIVITIES

The Smithsonian Institution

John Quincy Adams played a major role in setting up the Smithsonian Institution. In a corner of the classroom have students make a Smithsonian-type display. Students can display coin collections, stamp collections, insects, or historic mementos, much like the real Smithsonian.

Children of Presidents

If the child of a president ran for office, would the parent's popularity or lack of it affect the son's or daughter's chances for success? Briefly identify the following people for the students. Then run three mock elections. After the elections, ask students if the presidential parent of the candidate affected how they voted.

George W. Bush   vs.   Chelsea Clinton (as adult)

Julie Nixon Eisenhower   vs.   Jack Ford
(daughter of Richard Nixon)   (son of Gerald Ford)

Amy Carter   vs.   Michael Reagan
(daughter of Jimmy Carter)   (son of Ronald Reagan)

Retired Presidents

Assign teams to research what America's living former presidents are now doing. If there are not enough living presidents, then research what the five most recent presidents did in retirement. Biographies of former presidents or biographies of former first ladies are good places to look. When students finish reporting to the class, everybody might vote on which presidents made the best use of their retirement years.

Andrew Jackson (page 19)

Answer key: 1, 3, 4, 5

CLASS DISCUSSION

1. Andrew Jackson was a complicated man. Many people loved him and many hated him. Jackson himself was a man of strong love and deep hatred. What were his best qualities and what were his worst? Do you think a man like Jackson could be elected president today? Why? Why not?

2. By the time Jackson became president, he carried two bullets in his body from dueling. Some doctors feared these bullets were slowly poisoning him. He suffered from constant headaches, dysentery, kidney trouble, and bronchial trouble. Should a presidential candidate be required to undergo a physical examination so the public knows his or her condition? Why or why not? Do you think Jackson's health affected any of his decisions? Explain.

GROUP ACTIVITIES

Trail of Tears Mural

Have students make a mural of the Trail of Tears. First have students look at paintings of the Trail of Tears in history textbooks or books about the Native-American experience. Then have each member of the class draw an Indian man, woman, or child, or a farm animal or wagon. On a large sheet of paper attached to one wall of the classroom, paint a background of the landscape found along the route the Southeast Indians took—the flat/hilly lands of Alabama, or the grasslands of Arkansas and Oklahoma. Glue the student-drawn figures on the mural as they probably looked heading west.

Jackson's Ways

Organize the class into groups to discuss what might have happened in the two following situations if Jackson had been president.

1. When the U.S. Supreme Court ordered all American schools to admit all neighborhood children into the same school without regard to their race, would Jackson have carried out the Supreme Court's order? Why or why not?

2. When it seemed the only way to quickly end World War II was to drop an atomic bomb on the two Japanese cities of Hiroshima and Nagasaki, would Jackson have decided to drop the bomb or not? Explain.

Groups should report their conclusions to the class.

Jackson Posters

Organize the class into teams to research some of the anti-Jackson and pro-Jackson comments of that era. Have students make up colorful anti-Jackson posters denouncing him as an ignorant firebrand, and pro-Jackson posters describing him as a romantic buckskin frontier hero. Some students might want to write catchy jingles or slogans as well.

Martin Van Buren (page 22)

Answer key: law, magician, Panic, slavery, man

CLASS DISCUSSION

1. Martin Van Buren, at 5 feet 6 inches, was not very tall. Would that be more of a problem today than it was in his time? What would the shorter candidate do during television debates when each candidate stands at a podium? In most elections the taller candidate has won the election. Why do you think this is? Are there ways to make height less important?

2. Van Buren was not a popular president. Do you think the popularity of a president is based on how well the country is doing, or on personal characteristics of the president? What qualities about Van Buren do you think people found unattractive?

GROUP ACTIVITIES

The Big Moment: A Survey

Van Buren always remembered his chance to speak in court as the turning point in his life. Have students interview adults in their lives to see if any remember a special big moment that proved a turning point in their lives. Ask students to write down those incidents and share them with the class.

Bed of Roses/Bed of Thorns

Van Buren always wanted to be president. He called the presidency "the glittering prize." Have students think of other terms that might describe the presidency, both positive and negative. Suggest to students phrases describing the power and responsibility of the job. Collect the best phrases and make a poster using them.

Hat Thief on Trial: One-Act Play

Ask students to write a simple scene depicting a person caught wearing a hat that was just stolen from a store. Select students to play the judge, defense lawyer, prosecutor, accused thief, and storekeeper. In the play, the student playing the accused and the student playing the defense lawyer should work out a reasonable explanation for why he or she was wearing the stolen hat. The students playing the defense lawyer and the prosecutor should make summaries as young Van Buren did. Have the class vote for the best summary.

William Henry Harrison (page 25)

Answer key: 1. b   2. c   3. a   4. e   5. d

CLASS DISCUSSION

1. William Henry Harrison didn't like having to push the Native Americans off their lands. But he followed orders. Was he wrong in doing his duty as a soldier even if he didn't approve of what was going on? If a soldier or a commander followed his own heart concerning right and wrong, could an army work?

2. Harrison was sixty-eight when he became president. Ronald Reagan was sixty-nine when he was elected the first time and seventy-three the second time. Reagan finished his term and remained active long after leaving office, but Harrison died about a month after becoming president. Should there be an age limit on presidents?

GROUP ACTIVITIES

Tecumseh vs. Harrison: A Dialogue

Have students research Tecumseh and Harrison. Then ask several student volunteers to prepare a speech presenting the point of view of either Tecumseh or Harrison. Have students audition to play the two individuals. Then have the two selected students give their speeches. Ask the class to vote on which was most persuasive.

Tippecanoe and Tyler Too: Slogans

Harrison's campaign slogan was "Tippecanoe and Tyler too." Ask the class to compose catchy and colorful slogans for the first nine presidents. Jingles could substitute for slogans. Make a bulletin board display of the best slogans and jingles.

Wagons West: Dramatization

In 1841, the year Harrison became president, the first emigrant train, with forty-seven people, left Independence, Missouri. Divide the class in half. Have one half help make a large wall mural showing western landscapes and a large covered wagon. Have the other half research what life was like along the trails. Then have members of the research group arrange themselves in front of the wall mural and play the roles of men, women, and children who went west. After identifying themselves, they should simply tell what happened based on their research. For example, a student playing a young girl might say, "I am Emily Hartsworth, age twelve. Our wagon train was caught in a rainstorm, and we almost drowned crossing a swollen river. We lost many of our possessions."

John Tyler (page 28)

Answer key: 1. teacher   2. federal   3. Texas   4. Sherwood Forest   5. traitor

CLASS DISCUSSION

1. Tyler believed his slaves were happy at Sherwood Forest. He was a kind master; his slaves had plenty to eat and a decent place to live. Since Tyler felt they would be satisfied with this arrangement, what does this tell you about Tyler's attitudes? What do you think he thought about his slaves? Did he like them, hate them, or look down upon them?

2. Tyler was the first person to reach the presidency after a president died in office. People had little respect for him because of how he became president. Is this still the case? Do we treat a person who "accidentally" becomes president any differently than an elected president?

GROUP ACTIVITIES

John Tyler: A Mock Trial

Have the class conduct a trial of John Tyler for treason. Help students choose a judge, a jury, a committee for the prosecution, and a committee for the defense. Have the students research the background of the accusations against Tyler as well as arguments for his defense. Students should prepare the case carefully and then carry out the trial. The jury decides his guilt or innocence.

Don't Mess with Texas

Tyler wanted to annex Texas, and Texas joined the Union shortly after he left office. The slogan "Don't mess with Texas" warns today's Texans and visitors alike not to damage the state's environment. Assign teams of students to various regions of Texas: Coastal Plain, Great Plains, North Central Plains, Basin and Range Region, and rivers and lakes. Have the teams make murals showing drawn, painted, or photocopied pictures of each region. Then have the entire class compose other catchy environmental slogans that might be used to preserve the beauty of Texas.

Life As a Slave

Have students form teams to research life as a slave. The research should not focus on the brutality of the slave experience, but on the ordinary regimen, such as the lack of freedom to move to another location, do another kind of work, marry a person of one's choice, etc. Then have teams present the information in brief reports. Some students may wish to make posters showing the everyday experiences of slaves. These might be illustrated with photocopied pictures from library books.

James K. Polk (page 31)

Answer key: (a) 5   (b) 2   (c) 1   (d) 3   (e) 4

CLASS DISCUSSION

1. James Polk was an unknown person to most Americans when he became president. What do you see as the greatest advantage of a little-known new president? What would be a disadvantage? Do you think it's good that occasionally a newcomer appears from nowhere and becomes president? Why or why not?

2. During the Mexican War, the American Army got as far as Mexico City in the south. What if President Polk had decided to keep all that territory? What do you think would have happened? Do you think that someday the United States, Mexico, and Canada will merge as one country? Why or why not?

GROUP ACTIVITIES

Eyewitness News at Guadalupe Hidalgo Signing

Have the class research the terms of the Treaty of Guadalupe Hidalgo that ended the Mexican War. Then have students imagine they are a news crew reporting on this significant moment. Ask several students to play the reporters and present a news account of the treaty to the class. Other class members will act as people on the street whom reporters will ask to state their opinion about the treaty terms. Reporters may wish to hold an improvised microphone as they go from person to person.

Interviewing President Polk

Have students imagine they are in a press corps chosen to ask President Polk a question. Each student should do research and prepare five questions. Each student will ask only one question. The backup questions may be needed if students prepare some of the same questions. Ask three students to volunteer to play Polk;

two assistants can answer the questions as the Polk administration probably would have.

The Mexican War: A Debate

Have the class research the Mexican War and then conduct a debate on it according to instructions on page *vii*.

Zachary Taylor (page 34)

Answer key: 1. True   2. False   3. False   4. True   5. False

CLASS DISCUSSION

1. Our first president, George Washington, ran a farm, surveyed land, and did many other things in addition to being a soldier. But Zachary Taylor spent his entire adult life as a soldier. Do you think this was good preparation for being president? Why would a person accustomed to the army, giving and taking orders, find the presidency frustrating?

2. Do you feel Taylor enjoyed a good childhood? Would you have liked to live in that place and time? What parts of his childhood appeal to you and which do not? Where in America today might children have equally frightening experiences as Taylor had?

GROUP ACTIVITIES

Seminole Homeland Mural

Have students make a large mural depicting the old Seminole homeland along Lake Okeechobee. The mural might depict palm trees and Seminole houses—simple frame homes plastered with red clay and covered with roofs made of tree bark. Each student might draw a house or a palm tree, cut it out, and glue it to the mural.

The Gold Rush

The gold rush in California took place during Taylor's term. Assign teams of three or four students to research the gold rush and answer the following questions:

(a) What were some of the names of the gold rush towns? What were the towns like?

(b) What were the prices of everyday items, such as coffee, apples, bread, eggs, and newspapers? How do these prices compare to today's prices for the same items?

(c) How successful were most of the gold miners? How did they work? What tools did they use?

(d) Who were the vigilantes? How did they work?

Have the teams report their findings to the class. Encourage them to make use of visual aids, such as posters depicting prices of items or photocopied scenes of gold mining towns.

Zachary Taylor Portraits

Have the students find various paintings of Zachary Taylor. Then have them do some research in biographies, history textbooks, and other sources to find out what Zachary Taylor actually looked like. In real life Taylor often wore old farm clothing and sat on his horse sideways. Ask students to compare how Taylor actually looked with how he was depicted in paintings. Do the paintings flatter the president?

Millard Fillmore (page 37)

Answer key: 1. clothmaker   2. lawyer   3. California   4. Irish Catholics   5. Maryland

CLASS DISCUSSION

1. In Fillmore's time, many boys were apprentices. They lived with a master craftsman and learned a trade such as shoemaking or ironworking at about age fourteen. Do you think this was a good idea? Should boys and girls today have the opportunity to end school at fourteen and begin learning a trade?

2. Fillmore joined the American, or Know-Nothing, Party, which was against immigrants. Even though most American families were originally immigrants, there is often a feeling against the newer immigrants. Why do you think this is?

GROUP ACTIVITIES

Americans All

Ask all students to write on a slip of paper the country where their ancestors were born. Some students may need help—if they are Irish American, the country would be Ireland, and so on. If a student's ancestors came from two countries, both should be included. If a student was born in a foreign country, he or she should name the country. Students should not sign these slips. Have students drop all the slips in a basket. Then have the class work in groups to make a display showing flags of each ancestor country. Students will find the flags in a large atlas or encyclopedia.

Top Books

Millard Fillmore's home contained three books—the Bible, a hymn book, and an almanac. Ask each member of the class to write on a blank slip of paper (no student names) what five books should be in every home. Compile a list of the top favorites and post it on the bulletin board. (You may wish to allow students to get their parents' input for the lists, and name their books the following day.)

Reader's Theater

Uncle Tom's Cabin was published during Fillmore's term. Ask a group of students to work together to create a one-act play based on a chapter from *Uncle Tom's Cabin*. After the play has been presented to the class, have students discuss insights they have learned from the play.

Franklin Pierce (page 40)

Answer key: (a) 4   (b) 2   (c) 1   (d) 5   (e) 3

CLASS DISCUSSION

1. Franklin Pierce studied law and later became a soldier. What is there about being a lawyer that might seem a good career choice for a young person today? What is there about being in the military service that would appeal to a young person today? What features of following the law or the military life are attractive or unattractive?

2. Do you think forcing young Pierce to remain at Hancock Academy made him a stronger person? If a parent requires a son or daughter to stick with a disagreeable duty, do you think the child will have a better chance of being a successful adult? Why or why not?

GROUP ACTIVITIES

Not Made in the U.S.A.: A Survey

Remind students that Pierce opened Japan to American trade. Today we are more likely to own something made in Japan, or another foreign nation, than in the U.S.A. We buy more foreign products than most people in foreign countries buy American products—which has resulted in a trade deficit. To help students understand the trade deficit, have them inventory items in and around their own homes, including family automobiles. Provide each member of the class with a tabulation sheet with spaces to list items and the countries where they were made. Students should not put their names on the sheets. Tabulate the results of the survey, and write them on the board or post them on the bulletin board. Briefly explain to students how what they have found explains the trade deficit.

Kansas-Nebraska Act: A Debate

Have students research and debate the merits of the Kansas-Nebraska Act. If it had been carried out as planned, with honest elections, would it have ended the debate over slavery? For guidelines on conducting debates, refer to page *vii*.

Kansas Election: A Dramatization

Review with students the events surrounding the Kansas-Nebraska Act, including the dishonest voting that took place. Designate eight students as official residents of Kansas with the right to vote. Give them a special slip of paper on which is written "Resident of Kansas." Set up a voting booth and prepare ballots with these choices: (1) A free Kansas; (2) Slavery allowed in Kansas. Assign a student to pass out ballots to official voters (and privately inform the other students that anybody can vote). Tabulate the results, and point out that while eight were qualified to vote, tabulated votes add up to a much higher number.

James Buchanan (page 43)

Answer key: 1,   4

CLASS DISCUSSION

1. Do you think a president who always takes the middle ground on issues to please all sides can ever be successful? Can such a president be most successful if no great national problems are before the nation? Do you feel a president like Buchanan could be very popular? Explain your answers.

2. Buchanan never married. Would being single make it harder or easier to be president? What are the advantages and disadvantages? What circumstances would be difficult for a single president? What circumstances might make it very hard for a married president to concentrate on world problems?

GROUP ACTIVITIES

Log Cabin Project

Have students work in groups to research log cabins in encyclopedias and other reference books. Then have each group prepare a working drawing of a log cabin to be posted in class.

Secession Debate

Have students research how people living in South Carolina felt about secession. Why did some people want to leave the United State and others want to remain in the Union? Have students debate the secession issue from the point of view of South Carolinians before the Civil War. For guidelines on conducting a debate, refer to page *vii*.

Secession: Why?

Organize the class into teams to research each state that seceded from the Union. Each team should determine whether its assigned state was a major slaveholding state and, if not, why it seceded. Have teams share the results of their research with the class.

Abraham Lincoln (page 46)

Answer key: 1. True   2. False   3. True   4. False   5. True

CLASS DISCUSSION

1. What do you think the United States would be like today if the Civil War had not been fought? Would the southern states that left the Union still be a separate country? Would the United States be an ally of that country? Would there be serious disagreements between the two countries? Or do you think the states that seceded would have returned to the Union?

2. The Civil War was called a war between brothers. Many families were divided, with some sons and brothers fighting on the Union side and others on the Confederate side. Why would such a war be more bitter than a war between strangers? Do you think the war caused permanent rifts in families?

GROUP ACTIVITIES

Civil War Poetry

Many poems about Lincoln were written during and after the Civil War. Have student volunteers read aloud to the class such poems as "O Captain, My Captain" by Walt Whitman, "Abraham Lincoln Walks at Midnight" by Vachel Lindsay, and "Lincoln, Man of the People" by Edwin Markham. Have students share insights they have gained from the poetry. Some students may wish to write their own poems about Lincoln.

Lincoln and Douglas Dialogue

Have students work in groups to write an imaginary dialogue between Lincoln and Douglas, either before or after the famous debate. Members of each group should choose readers to present their dialogue to the class.

Civil War Battlefields

Ask students to refer to a historic atlas or history text to list the major battles of the Civil War. Assign each battlefield to a group of students; have the group find out what's happening at the site today. Groups might also look at famous paintings of their assigned battlefield, such as Winslow Homer's *A Skirmish in the Wilderness*, (Wilderness Campaign) and James Walker's painting of Lookout Mountain. They might also obtain photographs of these battlefields, such as the powerful pictures of Gettysburg, and either photocopy them for a poster or paint an original picture using the photograph as a model.

Andrew Johnson (page 49)

Answer key: (a) 4   (b) 2   (c) 1   (d) 5   (e) 3

CLASS DISCUSSION

1. Do you believe a man like Andrew Johnson, with his lack of education and rough ways, could be elected president today? Why or why not? Do you think such a person could make a good president today, or does today's world require a more educated person? Think about some recent presidents. Do you think they were all more competent than Andrew Johnson? Explain your answer.

2. One vote saved Johnson from impeachment. Impeachment is the only way to remove a president in the United States. In Great Britain, when most people think a prime minister is doing a poor job, that person can be removed by a vote of "no confidence." Would that system work here? Would you favor such a system?

GROUP ACTIVITIES

Alaska

In 1867 Johnson purchased Alaska for about $7,000,000. Organize students into teams to research the answers to these questions:

1. How has Alaska added to the wealth of America?

2. What are the unique natural wonders of Alaska?

3. What kinds of people lived in Alaska in 1867?

When teams complete their research, have them report their findings to the class. Encourage teams to use visual aids such as videos or colorful posters.

Irish and Chinese Railroad Builders

During Johnson's term, the Union Pacific and Central Pacific railroads were completed. They finally linked in 1869 at Promontary, Utah. Irish and Chinese immigrants did most of the work. Have students research the building of the railroad and make a large class display of photocopied or drawn pictures.

or

Greatest American Woman

Ask students to imagine they are living in 1865 and must honor America's greatest woman of achievement. Have them research the following women and choose one to honor with a poster.

Maria Mitchell   Harriet Beecher Stowe
Elizabeth Blackwell   Susan B. Anthony
Dorothea Lynd Dix

Ulysses S. Grant (page 52)

Answer key: 1. Horses   2. Washington   3. dishonest   4. Fort Donelson   5. Mexican War

CLASS DISCUSSION

1. General Grant wasn't a skillful general, but he never gave up. Because of Grant's tactic of fighting on, many of his men died. Some criticized Grant for being willing to lose so many men. Does being a good general mean putting winning ahead of

everything else? Or should a general put the welfare of his troops first? Explain your answer.

2. What personal character weaknesses do you think Grant had that allowed so many dishonest men to take over his administration?

GROUP ACTIVITIES

Civil War Songs

Play for the class recordings of Civil War songs like "Dixie," "Battle Hymn of the Republic," "Lorena," and others. After students hear the songs, have them discuss their reactions. Or have them work in groups to design a video show that uses specific songs as background for the pictures.

A Moral Decision: One-Act Play

Grant wouldn't turn against the dishonest people in his administration. Describe the following situation to students:

The treasurer of your ecology club is your best friend. On three different occasions, money for projects has vanished. Everybody suspects your friend, and you do too.

Select students to play the roles of the accused and three accusers. Have the students write dialogue in which the accusers present good evidence and the accused denies the charge. Then have them read their dialogue. Ask the rest of the class to vote on what to do—remain loyal to the treasurer, or expel him or her from the club. Members of the class should vote as if the treasurer were *their* best friend.

Grant—Success or Failure: A Debate

Have the class research Grant and then debate whether he was a success or failure as a general and as president. Refer to the debate instructions on page *vii* for guidelines.

Rutherford B. Hayes (page 55)

Answer key: 1. b   2. c   3. a   4. c   5. d

CLASS DISCUSSION

1. Do you think Hayes's early experience of being overprotected made him a stronger or a weaker person? Or did it make no difference? What do you think formed Hayes's character? What family member probably had the greatest influence? Why?

2. Right after the Civil War, African Americans enjoyed many rights, including voting and being elected to office. Then, after 1876, the southern states passed new laws severely restricting these rights. Why do you think this happened? Why, more than ten years after the Civil War, did the white southerners try to put black southerners into a lower place in society?

GROUP ACTIVITIES

Lemonade Lucy: A Display

Lucy Hayes was a strong-minded first lady. She was nicknamed "Lemonade Lucy" because she refused to serve liquor at the White House. She was notable in several other ways, as well. She promoted good causes—like stopping child labor abuse, and opposing discrimination against African Americans. She also started the tradition of the Easter egg roll on the White House lawn. Have students photocopy pictures that honor Lucy Hayes for her achievements.

Jim Crow Laws

Organize the class into teams to research Jim Crow laws. Then have students create a large photocopied or drawn display showing the many signs throughout the South that reminded African Americans they were considered a lower class.

Election of 1876

Choose two teams to research the election of 1876. Then have them form a Hayes campaign committee and a Tilden campaign committee. Have them conduct a campaign featuring speeches made by students chosen by their campaign committee to role-play Hayes and Tilden. The campaign should also include posters, appropriate slogans, and perhaps some red, white, and blue balloons. After the campaign, have a mock election.

James A. Garfield (page 58)

Answer key: Guiteau, Garfield, Garfield, Guiteau, Guiteau, Garfield

CLASS DISCUSSION

1. President Garfield became a teacher at age eighteen. Some of his students were sixteen and very tough. Garfield was physically attacked by them, and he fought back in hand-to-hand combat. What would happen if a teacher today did the same? What should Garfield have done when confronted by a violent student intent on beating him up?

2. Garfield never had time to show what kind of a president he might have been. But if he had had the time to serve for a full term, which of his earlier experiences do you think would have helped him the most? He was a farmer, he worked on a cargo ship, he taught, and he fought in the Civil War. What do you think each of these experiences taught him?

GROUP ACTIVITIES

Capital Punishment: A Debate

In 1882, Charles Guiteau was executed for assassinating President Garfield. Have students debate whether or not Guiteau should have been executed and whether or not capital punishment is acceptable or desirable. Refer to page *vii* for guidelines on how to conduct a debate.

Booker T. Washington

When Garfield was president, Booker T. Washington founded Tuskegee Institute to train African Americans to be successful. Have the class research Washington's accomplishments and then prepare a display to honor him. This could include the postage stamp bearing his likeness, photocopies and sketches of Tuskegee Institute, and pictures of notable graduates of Tuskegee.

McGuffey Readers

When Garfield was a teacher, McGuffey Readers were commonly used as textbooks. The stories in these readers were used not only to teach reading, but also to teach morality. Find copies of this once-popular reader and share them with the students. Have students do one of the following:

1. Write an original story that teaches the values of kindness, generosity, or truthfulness.

2. Find and share a short story from a modern reader that teaches such values. Or, working with a partner, change a modern story to include a "moral," making it more like a McGuffey Reader story.

Chester Arthur (page 61)

Answer key: 1. b   2. a   3. c   4. a   5. d

CLASS DISCUSSION

1. It was said of Arthur that he "looked like a president." How important is this? Is it more important now than it was in Arthur's time? Do we respect our presidents on the basis of how dignified they look, or by how much they seem like regular people?

2. Arthur was a widower with a ten-year-old daughter when he moved to the White House. What do you think are the good and bad parts of being a child in the White House? Do you think it's easier or harder for a child to grow up in the White House today than it was when Arthur's daughter lived there? Why?

GROUP ACTIVITIES

American Red Cross: A Display

The American Red Cross was founded in 1881, the year Arthur became president. Have students make a class display featuring photos of recent Red Cross relief work in floods, earthquakes, etc. Have them photocopy or clip out pictures from newspapers, or have them make drawings.

The Merit System: A Debate

Have the class research and debate the merit system versus the spoils system. Refer to the guidelines for conducting a debate on page *vii*.

A Streetcar Ride: One-Act Play

Have a group of students write dialogue for a one-act play based on the Lizzie Jennings incident. Members of the group should be selected to play Jennings, the streetcar conductor, and several other passengers who might have commented as she attempted to board the streetcar. After the rest of the students have seen the play, ask them to discuss what cash settlement might have been fair to Jennings. (It is not known how much she did get, but she was very pleased with the amount.)

Grover Cleveland (page 64)

Answer key: 1. b   2. c   3. d   4. b   5. a

CLASS DISCUSSION

1. What qualities did Grover Cleveland display as a young man that showed he might one day make a good leader? If you had known young Cleveland, would you have admired him? Why or why not?

2. It was said of Cleveland, "We love him for the enemies he has made." Do you think it is possible to be an effective leader without ever making an enemy? Describe some issues on which good people might strongly disagree.

GROUP ACTIVITIES

Statue of Liberty: A Display

Divide the class into groups to prepare a display honoring the Statue of Liberty, which was dedicated in 1866 by President Cleveland. Groups could read about and prepare a display on how the monument was built; who gave it to the U.S. and why; and the life of Emma Lazarus, who wrote "The New Colossus," which appears on the monument. To dedicate the display, students could read aloud assigned lines of the poem "The New Colossus."

Election of 1884

The election of 1884 was one of the nation's dirtiest because of a mudslinging campaign. Have teams of students research the campaign and then make posters and print slogans on placards. Have the students hold a mock rally for each of the candidates in which they feature the mudslinging slogans. Then have students hold a mock election.

1885–1889—Spotlight on the News

Have students look up and research some major world events that took place during the years of Cleveland's presidency. Be sure they include:

1885—Germany seizes Marshall and Solomon Islands
        Congo Free State established by Belgium's King Leopold
1886—Haymarket riots
        Apache Chief Geronimo surrenders
1889—Johnstown flood
        Brazil becomes a republic

Organize the class into teams to deliver eyewitness news reports of the events.

Benjamin Harrison (page 67)

Answer key: 1. President   2. Indian wars   3. cold as an iceberg   4. Chile   5. tariffs

CLASS DISCUSSION

1. When Ben Harrison was a child, his grandfather was the president. What would be the advantages and disadvantages of having a grandparent in the White House? Do you think such a grandchild would share the popularity or unpopularity of the grandparent in office? Would it be dangerous? In what way?

2. Some people described Harrison as "cold as an iceberg." Could such a person be elected president today? If elected, could such a person be a good president? In what ways might such a president be more effective than a warm, friendly person?

GROUP ACTIVITIES

A Tariff Demonstration

High tariffs were a big issue during Harrison's term. Briefly explain what a tariff is and then arrange for a demonstration. Position one student at a desk labeled "Foreign-made," and another at a desk labeled "American-made." Give each student five identical items (for example, five transistor radios to the American desk, five to the foreign). American radios will be priced around $20. Foreign radios should be priced around $18. Assign another student to be a tax official who adds $3 to each of the foreign-made radios. As a culminating activity, ask students to answer these questions:

Are tariffs good for American workers?
Are tariffs good for American consumers?

High/Low Tariffs: A Debate

Have students debate the merits of high tariffs versus low tariffs. Refer to page *vii* for instructions on conducting debates.

First Ladies: A Mural

Caroline Lavinia Harrison was a great help to her husband and a remarkable person in her own right. Have students work in teams to research the lives of the first ladies up to Mrs. Harrison and feature their accomplishments on a mural. The mural should include symbols and photocopied pictures that represent the women and their accomplishments. For example, Caroline Harrison was a fine watercolor artist. Martha Washington joined her husband at Valley Forge to help the soldiers. Louisa Adams (wife of John Quincy Adams) raised silkworms. Abigail Powers Fillmore was a teacher. Frances Folsom Cleveland managed to make the White House a happy home for her small children.

William McKinley (page 70)

Answer key: soldier, teacher, governor, lawyer

CLASS DISCUSSION

1. Young McKinley was always reading books. Do you think this helped him when he became president? How? Does a president have to do a lot of reading in office? What if the president just doesn't like reading long reports? Can the job of president still be done effectively?

2. McKinley was forced into the Spanish-American War by hysteria whipped up by the press. Do you think today's television stories could whip up enough public feeling to force the current president into a war that isn't in the nation's best interests?

GROUP ACTIVITIES

Stop the Tyrant: Campaign for Action

Have a team of students invent an imaginary country ruled by a cruel tyrant. This tyrant is persecuting the people and arresting them without cause. Refugees from this country are streaming into neighboring countries.

Have other members of the class form into teams to publicize this situation. One team might prepare a graphic report telling the stories of survivors (students may play the roles of survivors). Another team might prepare a wall display showing tragic photos of fleeing refugees or victims of persecution (may be photocopied from recent trouble spots in the world). Culminate the activity with a class vote on whether or not America should intervene to depose the tyrant.

Who Sank the *Maine*? An Inquiry

Organize the class into teams to research the sinking of the *Maine*. Teams should read library books and gather evidence. When the teams have finished their research, have them report their findings to the class. The class then votes on the following probabilities:

Resolved: Spain probably sank the *Maine*.
Spain probably did not sink the *Maine*.
We really don't know why the *Maine* sank.

McKinley's Death: Presidents at Risk

Have student teams research the assassinations of Lincoln, Garfield, and McKinley and the attempted assassination of President Theodore Roosevelt. Then have the teams recommend ways presidents could be made more safe.

Theodore Roosevelt (page 73)

Answer key: 1. c   2. d   3. d   4. a   5. c

CLASS DISCUSSION

1. Roosevelt liked to say "Speak softly and carry a big stick." What does this mean? Is it good national policy? Describe concrete situations where this would be done, using current world trouble spots.

2. Roosevelt was a weak and sickly boy. How did he react to his physical condition? What do you think his future might have been like if he had not taken the course of action he did? Do you think overcoming being weak and frail made him a stronger president than if he had been a strong and husky youth?

GROUP ACTIVITIES

Roosevelt's Letters

When Roosevelt was away from home, he sent illustrated letters to all his children about subjects he thought would interest them. Have students look through the book *Theodore Roosevelt's Letters to His Children* (Joseph Bocklin Bishop, Editor. New York: A Signet Classic, 1964). Then have students write an illustrated letter to younger siblings or a younger friend. Students not adept at art might illustrate their letters with colorful stickers. Have students share their letters with the class.

National Parks: A Display

Have the class make a display of national parks and monuments as a tribute to Roosevelt's environmental achievements. Students should include Mount Rushmore, which bears his likeness. The display might consist of photocopied pictures from books and magazines.

Nobel Peace Prize: A Nomination

Theodore Roosevelt won the Nobel Peace Prize. He was the first president to win it and, as of 1996, Woodrow Wilson has been the only other one. Ask students to form teams to research contributions to peace made by Presidents Nixon, Ford, Carter, Reagan, Bush, and Clinton. Have each team then nominate one of these presidents for a Nobel Peace Prize. Ask volunteers to make a poster announcing the president who got the vote from most groups. If there was a tie, both names should appear on the poster.

William Howard Taft *(page 76)*

Answer key: lawyer, judge, governor

CLASS DISCUSSION

1. Taft never wanted to be president. Do you think a person who truly does not want to be president can still be a good president? Or do you think that not wanting the job can actually make a person a better president?

2. Do you think Taft was a popular child? What qualities could you have found appealing in a friend like him? What was there about Willie that might have made him unpopular?

GROUP ACTIVITIES

Supreme Court: A Review

Have the class work in groups to research the activities and accomplishments of the last five Chief Justices of the Supreme Court. Then have the groups report their findings to the class. After hearing all the reports, the entire class votes on who they think was the most effective.

Taft vs. Teddy Roosevelt: A Dialogue

The friendship between Taft and Teddy Roosevelt ended when Taft became president. Assign a team to research Taft's side of the controversy and another to research Roosevelt's side. Each team should then choose a speaker to act as the president the team has researched. The two "presidents" take part in a dialogue that presents the two positions. Once both speakers have explained why the feud was the other's fault, have the class vote on who they feel the guilty party was.

Panama Canal: A Research Project

As head of the War Department under President Roosevelt, Taft led the building of the Panama Canal. One of the marvels of the New World, the Panama Canal is still an engineering wonder. Divide the class into groups to research the canal. Direct half of the groups to prepare a large wall display featuring pictures of the canal, photocopied from books and magazines, and a map showing exactly where it is. Tell the other groups to work together to prepare large drawings showing how the canal locks operate. Students will find diagrams showing the profile of the Panama Canal and its locks in most encyclopedias.

Woodrow Wilson (page 79)

Answer key: 1. c   2. d   3. c   4. d   5. c

CLASS DISCUSSION

1. Part of Wilson's New Freedom program was curbing child labor. How old do you think a young person should be before being permitted to work without special safety precautions and limitations on hours? What, if any, advantages does child labor offer society and children? What are the drawbacks of child labor to society and children?

2. World War I was called by some "the war to end all wars." It clearly was not that. Do you think wars ever make future wars less likely? Or does war *always* beget new wars? If a war is likely to bring future peace, what kind of a peace should be imposed on the loser? If the peace terms are harsh, are new wars more likely? Explain.

GROUP ACTIVITIES

The *Lusitania*: A Research Inquiry

During Wilson's presidency, the passenger ship *Lusitania* was sunk by Germans because it carried weapons. Many innocent civilians, including Americans, died. Have students research the sinking of the *Lusitania* and prepare a pictorial display about it. You may wish to read to the class portions of Colin Simpson's *The Lusitania* (Boston: Little, Brown, 1972) and allow students to peruse the book. The display should include reproduced pictures related to the sinking of the *Lusitania*. There are some excellent possibilities in Simpson's book, including shrapnel loaded in the bottom of the ship (p. 104), a dramatic scrap of paper bearing the ship's last message (p. 203), and poignant photographs of victims and graves.

League of Nations: A Debate

Have students research the pros and cons of the United States joining the League of Nations at the time of Wilson's presidency. Then have students debate the issue. For guidelines on conducting a debate, refer to page *vii*.

Honoring Edith Wilson

Edith Wilson saw her husband, the president, incapacitated by arteriosclerosis and a thrombosis that paralyzed his left arm and leg. For two months, when he was between life and death, Mrs. Wilson played a large role in keeping the government running smoothly. Have student teams design and make posters honoring the courage and steadfastness of this woman.

Warren G. Harding (page 84)

Answer key: 1 . +   2. +   3. −   4. +   5. −

CLASS DISCUSSION

1. Harding appointed many personal friends to important jobs. Why was that not a good idea? Would it be easier to fire a poor employee who was not a friend? Why do you think Harding chose so many friends?

2. What do you think was Harding's big appeal when he was elected president? What was the mood of the American people? What did they long for?

GROUP ACTIVITIES

Slogans

Harding's slogan was "Back to Normalcy." Tell students to work with a partner to create a slogan better suited to his presidency. The slogan may be positive or negative. Have the class choose the five best slogans for posting on the bulletin board.

Ohio Gang

Assign groups of students to research the deeds of the following men and to report on their record: Attorney General Daugherty, Jess Smith of the Department of Justice, Postmaster Will Hays, Veterans Bureau Chief Charles Forbes, Secretary of the Interior Albert Fall, and Gaston Means of the Department of Justice.

A Presidential News Conference

Remind students that President Harding never got the chance to explain to the American people why he'd hired so many dishonest men, nor was he able to apologize to the American people for all the corruption. Have everyone in the class research the Harding administration. Then either appoint three students, or ask for volunteers to play Harding and two press secretaries. Have the rest of the students each write five questions they would like to ask the Harding administration. Allow each student to ask Harding and his assistants one question.

Calvin Coolidge (page 85)

Answer key: 1. – 2. + 3. – 4. + 5. +

CLASS DISCUSSION

1. When Coolidge was a small boy, shyness was a big problem. If he had never overcome this problem, could he have become president?

2. Coolidge gained popularity by saying that police officers had no right to strike because the public safety was involved. Do you agree? Is this also true of medical personnel and firefighters? Do they have the right to strike? If not, how can they gain fair working conditions?

GROUP ACTIVITIES

1920's Music and Style

Coolidge was president during the "roaring twenties." Play some music from this era—especially George Gershwin, Sigmund Romberg (*The Desert Song*), Cole Porter, Richard Rodgers, Jerome Kern (*Show Boat*), as well as jazz instrumentals. Have students write about their reaction to the music. Or have students work in groups to create a bulletin-board display showing the fashions of the era photocopied from books and magazines.

Modern First Ladies

Grace Coolidge was one of America's most admired women. Have students research in groups the activities of five modern first ladies and make reports to the class. Feature women who have worked hard for specific causes, such as Grace Coolidge's work with the deaf, Lady Bird Johnson's beautification campaign, Nancy Reagan's antidrug work, and Barbara Bush's literacy drive.

Swearing In: A One-Act Play

Most presidents are sworn into office amid much pomp and circumstance, but Coolidge was sworn into office by his father, a notary public, by the light of a coal lamp. Have students research the oath of office. Then select two students to play Coolidge and his father, holding the Bible in a reenactment of the swearing-in ceremony.

Herbert Hoover (page 88)

Answer key: 1. b   2. b   3. a   4. a   5. c

CLASS DISCUSSION

1. Hoover was a very poor boy who made good by his own brains and mighty efforts. Do you think this made it harder for him to understand the suffering of the vast numbers of unemployed during the Depression?

2. Imagine that Hoover had never been president. What do you think he might have accomplished with his life? Might he have been an even greater man? Are some great men just unfit for the presidency? Why?

GROUP ACTIVITIES

Eyewitness to the Depression: Reader's Theater

Select passages from the Studs Terkel book *Hard Times* for students to read. Then, from books and magazines, have students compile a large display of scenes of the Depression for the classroom.

Memories of the Depression: Interviews

Have students speak to older relatives and other older people about their memories of the Depression. A visit to a retirement home would yield many interesting stories. Tell students to take notes and report what they have learned to the class.

The Bonus March: A Dramatization

Have students research the tragic Bonus March incident of 1932. (A good account may be found in *Riots—U.S.A. 1765–1970* by Willard A. Heaps, pp. 131–137.) Have selected students describe what happened as if they were there. They should try to capture the frustration of the veterans at the plight they were in.

Franklin Delano Roosevelt (page 91)

Answer key: (a) 3   (b) 5   (c) 1   (d) 4   (e) 2

CLASS DISCUSSION

1. Young Roosevelt grew up a pampered rich boy with advantages undreamed of by ordinary young people. Yet he put into place the largest program in history to help the jobless, poor, retired, and disabled. How do you explain this? He was called by wealthy friends "a traitor to his class." What did they mean?

2. One of Roosevelt's most famous quotes was, "The only thing we have to fear is fear itself." What does this quote mean to you? Do you believe this statement is always true? In what instances could it be false, and even dangerous?

GROUP ACTIVITIES

Physically Challenged Americans: A Research Project

Have the students work in groups to research noted Americans who have accomplished great things despite serious physical challenges. They should include such people as Franklin Roosevelt, who was paralyzed by polio as a young man, Helen Keller, Senator Robert Dole, Charles Proteus Steinmetz, etc. Have them culminate the activity with a bulletin-board display of pictures of the subjects who were researched.

Social Security Firsthand

Roosevelt put in the Social Security System to provide a pension for retired, disabled, and dependent families. Ask the students to interview relatives and friends who collect Social Security about what it means to them. If students cannot find such people, have them form groups to study the Social Security program—and especially how Franklin Roosevelt himself viewed it. Then have the groups report their findings to the class.

Battlefields of World War II

Have groups of students refer to a historical atlas or U.S. history textbook to list major theaters of battle in World War II. Each group should focus on one of the following: European area, Pacific area, or North African area. Help groups find dramatic pictures to photocopy for a large wall display.

Harry S Truman (page 94)

Answer key: 1. b   2. c   3. d   4. b   5. b

CLASS DISCUSSION

1. President Truman never went to college. Do you think this made it more difficult for him to be president? Do you think a candidate who never went to college could be elected today? What are the most important things a person might learn in college that would be of use in the White House?

2. Which of Truman's experiences as a young person and adult do you think proved most beneficial to him when he reached the White House? Did he use his experience on the railroad, in the military, or as a storekeeper to most advantage? What did he probably gain from each experience?

GROUP ACTIVITIES

Atomic Bomb: A Debate

Have students research the decision to drop the atomic bombs on Japan. Then have students debate whether or not it was a good decision. For instructions on conducting a debate, refer to page *vii.*

Korean War Memorial

The Korean War took place during Truman's term. There is a Vietnam War Memorial in Washington, but no Korean War Memorial. Five million Americans served in the Korean War. Thirty-three thousand Americans died, and over 100,000 Americans were wounded in the war. Have the class work in groups to research the Korean War and then design a fitting war memorial. When all the designs are in, have the class choose the best. All designs should be posted.

The Cold War: Communism vs. the Free World

During Truman's administration, the Cold War began. Soon after World War II ended, the United States and the Soviet Union became bitter enemies. Why did this happen? Give students a brief overview of the beginning of the Cold War, when the Soviet Union tried to take over more nations in Europe. Ask students, working in groups, to research one of the most menacing figures of the Communist world, Joseph Stalin. Once the research is complete, have groups report to the class about Stalin.

Dwight D. Eisenhower (page 97)

Answer key: 1. True   2. True   3. False   4. False   5. False

CLASS DISCUSSION

1. Eisenhower was a great war leader. How do you think this prepared him to be president? He ran the military forces in one of the world's most massive campaigns, the Allied campaign in Europe. After doing this, what would frustrate him as president? In what ways would he find his job as president more difficult? And being a military leader, how do you think he'd run the White House?

2. The slogan "I like Ike" swept America during the 1950's. He was one of the nation's most beloved presidents. What do you think accounted for this? His war hero status? His appearance and manner? The spirit of the 1950's?

GROUP ACTIVITIES

THE 1950's: Portrait of an Era

The 1950's were a peaceful and interesting time. Have students ask adult relatives and friends who lived in the 1950's what it was like. Ask them to find recordings of music popular in this era and to build a memorabilia display of 1950's items (or photos of them). Items might include 45-rpm records, photos of 1950's teenagers, pink-poodle-appliqued sweaters, etc. After students have listened to the music and looked at the memorabilia, have them vote on this question.

Would you have liked to live in the 1950's?

Hawaii and Alaska

Have groups research facts about Hawaii and Alaska, which became states during Eisenhower's term. Have groups make two wall displays, one for each state, featuring drawings, photocopied pictures, and maps.

Showdown at Little Rock: One-Act Play

Have students research what happened at Little Rock, Arkansas, when African-American young people entered Central High School. After they have read about the violence and confrontation, ask a group of students to write a one-act play about two students—one white, one black—meeting in an empty classroom and trying to be friends. The dialogue for the play should emphasize how the parents of the two young people feel and how the students themselves feel. (Students should have learned during research that many white parents bitterly opposed desegregation;

while many black parents hoped desegregation would open new opportunities. If necessary, guide playwrights in this direction.)

John F. Kennedy *(page 100)*

Answer key: 1. Choate   2. World War II   3. Peace Corps   4. Lee Harvey Oswald   5. Cuba

CLASS DISCUSSION

1. Kennedy was the first Roman Catholic elected president. Many refused to vote for him because of his religion. He had to go before groups of people to promise that his religion would not keep him from being a good president. How important do you think the religious faith of a president is?

2. In 1960, when Kennedy ran for president, televised debates were introduced. Many people felt that this played a big part in the victory of Kennedy. Kennedy looked young and vigorous; Nixon looked haggard and unpleasant. Do you think TV debates give certain candidates an unfair advantage? How could this be prevented?

GROUP ACTIVITIES

Peace Corps: A Mural

Kennedy established the Peace Corps. You might write to the Peace Corps at 1990 K St. N.W., Washington, D.C. 20526 prior to this segment of study and get information on which countries now use Peace Corps members. Have students use photocopied pictures from books and magazines to create a large collage of scenes from various countries where the Peace Corps serves. Display the collage on a wall.

Cuban Missile Crisis: A Debate

Have groups of students research the Cuban missile crisis and then debate the following question:

Was the blockade the right decision?

Refer to page *vii* for instructions on conducting debates.

Jacqueline Kennedy: Grace Under Pressure

When President Kennedy was assassinated on November 22, 1963, most Americans were totally stunned. A president had not been assassinated in the United States for sixty-two years. The vast majority of Americans had never before lived through an assassination. Some people feared Kennedy had been killed by a foreign plot. Others had other conspiracy theories. The calm, dignified behavior of the young widow, Jacqueline Kennedy, did much to help the nation also respond to this tragedy with dignity and calm. Have students form groups, read about Jacqueline Kennedy, and then design a fitting bulletin board display featuring photocopied or actual photos.

Lyndon B. Johnson (page 103)

Answer key: 1. a   2. c   3. d   4. d   5. c

CLASS DISCUSSION

1. Lyndon Johnson often said, "Let us reason together." He believed even political enemies could agree to pass laws for the good of all if they only reasoned together. In recent years Democrats and Republicans have often not been able to work together; each side is more interested in making itself look good and the other side look bad. How can this problem be resolved?

2. Lyndon Johnson became unpopular because of the Vietnam War. American troops were in Vietnam to keep South Vietnam free of Communism. Johnson said it would be wrong to just pull out and let the country fall to Communism. But many Americans were dying in Vietnam, and there seemed to be no end in sight. What should the president have done?

GROUP ACTIVITIES

A Lady Bird Day: Beautification Project

Have the students form groups. Each group will decide what might be done to improve the looks of the school. This should be done in keeping with the spirit of Lady Bird Johnson's campaign to beautify America by planting flowers, trees, and shrubs and cleaning up. Ask the groups to report their ideas. Then have the class select the best and most feasible project.

War on Poverty Bulletin Board

Johnson declared war on poverty. He said he would end the tragedy of poverty for American families. Have students form groups to research the question: Did Johnson win the war on poverty? Students will need to refer to encyclopedias, almanacs, etc., to find out how the percentage of people living in poverty today compares with the 1960's. Have students culminate the activity with a bulletin-board display of recent photographs of poverty in America. These may be photocopied from books and magazines. Success stories, such as improved neighborhoods, might also be included in the display.

Helping Head Start

Johnson established Head Start schools for disadvantaged young children. Have students make some colorful picture books to be donated to a local Head Start project. Or contact Head Start to find out their needs; students might raise money for books and playground equipment or donate used books.

Richard M. Nixon (page 106)

Answer key: 1. c   2. c   3. a   4. c   5. d

CLASS DISCUSSION

1. Nixon had many outstanding qualities, yet he fell from power in a tragic way. From reading the text, can you find clues that the president would eventually make mistakes that would bring about his fall? What personality traits, if any, made it more likely he would get involved in something like Watergate?

2. What if Nixon had not resigned? He faced an impeachment trial that would have gone on for a long time. Do you think Nixon did the right thing by resigning and sparing the nation this? Why do you think Nixon resigned?

GROUP ACTIVITIES

Landing on the Moon: A Mural

During Nixon's presidency, on July 20, 1969, Americans landed on the moon. Have students make a class mural featuring pictures of the moon and drawings or pictures of spacecrafts and astronauts involved in the historic event. Students might also want to make replicas of the moon or spacecraft or to display items they have, such as commemorative medallions, postage stamps, etc.

Political Cartoons on Nixon

Nixon was an ideal subject for political cartoonists. No president in recent times has been the subject of more cartoons, most very negative. Have students form groups and look at newspapers and magazines between April 1973 and August 1974 to find the best cartoons. Display copies of the cartoons on the bulletin board.

Watergate: Why?

Have students form groups to research the Watergate incident. Tell them to find out:

What really happened?
Did Nixon cover it up?

Have groups discuss among themselves where Nixon went wrong. What should he have done? Finally, have each group report its conclusions to the class.

Gerald R. Ford (page 109)

Answer key: 1. False   2. True   3. False   4. False   5. True

CLASS DISCUSSION

1. What do you think there was about Gerald Ford's personality that helped heal the wounds of the Watergate years? Why was Ford a welcome change from Nixon? Do you think Ford was as clever or brilliant as Nixon? If not, did that matter?

2. President Ford pardoned former President Nixon for covering up the Watergate break-in; he may have lost his bid for reelection because of that. If he had not pardoned Nixon, we might have seen a former president go to prison. Do you think that would have been harmful to the country? What do you think other nations might have thought?

GROUP ACTIVITIES

Vietnam War: Overdue Thanks

The Vietnam War completely ended during Ford's term. The Vietnam War Memorial in Washington bears the names of those servicepeople who died there. It's a V-shaped wall bearing the names of over 58,000 Americans. Many people come there and leave a letter, a poem, a rose, or some other memento. They are all collected, catalogued, and saved. (In fact, a book of photographs showing some of the many items left at the Wall has been published. You might want to share *Offerings at the Wall: Artifacts from the Vietnam Memorial Collection*, by Thomas B. Allen, with your students. It is published by Turner Publishing, Inc.) Ask students: If you were standing at the wall and had to leave something, what would it be? Have students write a poem, draw a picture, or describe the memento they'd like to leave there. Post these along the classroom wall as the class's special memorial for a few days.

American Made: A Survey

During Ford's term there was a recession. Ford urged all Americans to go out and buy something made in America. Ask members of the class to conduct their own survey. Have them look for items their family has bought in the last year and determine how many were made in America. Then have students form groups to design posters, buttons, etc., urging consumers to "buy American."

Vietnam Today

Have students work in groups to research Vietnam today. What is going on there now? How is the economy? How are relations with the United States? When groups have found out all they can, ask them to report their findings to the class.

Jimmy Carter (page 112)

Answer key: 1. peanuts   2. Lillian Carter   3. Amy Carter   4. Shah   5. Egypt

CLASS DISCUSSION

1. Carter walked to his own inauguration. He sent his daughter to the local public school—instead of to one of the costly private schools where most politicians send their children. What message was he trying to send to the American people? Is a humble president good for the country?

2. Carter was a completely fresh face on the national scene when he ran for president. A few years prior to the election, the vast majority of Americans had never heard of him. Is this a good thing? Are politicians who are well known and have served many years in other offices better candidates because we know more about them? Or are newcomers better, because they have a clean slate and have made fewer friends and enemies in politics?

GROUP ACTIVITIES

Former Presidents Bulletin-Board Display

After leaving the White House, Carter became widely admired for spending his time building houses for poor Americans and for traveling around the world to resolve crisis situations. What do most former presidents do in retirement? Have students form groups to research the last five presidents and make a bulletin-board display showing their activities. They might photocopy pictures showing Carter building houses and other presidents engaging in recreation and other activities.

The Hostage Crisis

Ask students to form groups to research what happened during the hostage crisis. Then have each group appoint a member who will join with members of other groups in a committee. The committee will decide if President Carter handled the crisis wisely, then report to the class about their conclusions.

Image of America

During the hostage crisis, there were many television scenes of blindfolded American hostages being roughly handled by crowds screaming anti-American slogans. Scenes of the American flag and photos of President Carter being burned in Iran were shown around the world. Many Americans saw their country as being humiliated before the world. Have students ask adults they know how they felt during this crisis. Ask them to record the comments and report them to the class. Then ask students to answer for themselves if Americans now feel better about their country.

Ronald Reagan (page 115)

Answer key: (a) 2   (b) 4   (c) 1   (d) 5   (e) 3

CLASS DISCUSSION

1. Reagan was called the "great communicator," because he often came before the American people and made speeches everyone understood. He would deliberately use simple language. For example, instead of saying, "You have noticed that inflation has put many items out of your reach," he would say something like, "When you go down to the grocery store, that milk you want to buy costs too much." As a young man, Reagan was an actor and a sportscaster. He had a lot of experience in communication. Do you think a president's ability to communicate in simple language is very important? Why or why not?

2. Reagan asked this question of the American people before the election of 1980: Are you better or worse off than you were before Carter became president? If you are better off, vote for him. If not, vote for me. Is this the only basis we should use in voting for president? What other questions might we ask?

GROUP ACTIVITIES

Simplifying a Speech

Form the class into groups and photocopy a rather complicated speech of about one hundred words. It may be from the text of an actual speech, or you may wish to make up one. Pass a copy to each group; tell groups to simplify the speech as best they can. Each group should select a member to read the simplified speech to the class. The class will then vote on which was the best simplified speech.

Women in Power: A Bulletin Board

Reagan appointed the first woman to serve on the Supreme Court, Sandra Day O'Connor. Have students research prominent women politicians today and make a bulletin-board display, featuring pictures of each. The politician's name, title, and major accomplishment should appear under each picture. For example, a senator might have been responsible for helping to pass a law. As a culminating activity, take a class vote on which of these women may be most qualified to be president.

Are You Better Off? A Survey

Have students ask Reagan's "Are you better off today" question of adults they know, substituting the name of the current president for Carter. Have students report the responses to the class.

George Bush *(page 118)*

Answer key: 1. pilot   2. Panama   3. China   4. Kuwait   5. American economy

CLASS DISCUSSION

1. Bush was an excellent vice president who served President Reagan loyally for eight years. Vice presidents don't have a lot of dramatic things to do, and sometimes they are not very visible. Do you think being vice president is good preparation for president? Why or why not?

2. Dan Quayle, Bush's vice president, made some errors in speech. Many comedians began making fun of him. Some people believe the jokes got out of hand and ruined Quayle's image. Do you think it's good when comedians poke fun at our political leaders? Do you think it keeps the politicians from getting too proud? How can comedians be fair while still being funny?

GROUP ACTIVITIES

Iraq and Kuwait—Desert Storm

Have students form groups and research the Desert Storm campaign. Have them answer these questions based on their research:

Did America and its allies have the right to interfere when Iraq invaded Kuwait?
Was it a mistake not to finish the job and conquer Iraq?
Could America have prevented the invasion in the first place? If so, how?

Literacy Campaign: Barbara Bush

Barbara Bush, the president's wife, worked hard for literacy. Have student groups make colorful posters promoting the reading of books. Conduct a class vote to determine the best five posters.

Fading Bubble of Popularity: A Survey

Right after the United States and its allies won the Desert Storm campaign, there were huge parades featuring yellow ribbons all over America. George Bush was at the peak of his popularity. Then, the following year, he lost the election. Have students ask adult family members and other adults if their opinion of Bush changed in the year before the election. If so, why? Have students report responses to the class.

Bill Clinton (page 121)

Answer key: 1. b   2. a   3. c   4. d   5. a

CLASS DISCUSSION

1. When Clinton was a teenager, he met President Kennedy and was so inspired that he decided to enter politics. What qualities about Kennedy do you think so struck the imagination of this Arkansas boy?

2. Hillary Rodham Clinton has played a big role in her husband's career. During the campaign of 1992 many Americans resented the fact that she seemed too strong and was not interested in domestic things (like baking cookies). Some people found her threatening; others loved her strong style. Do you think it is proper for the president's spouse to play a big role in the administration? Why or why not?

GROUP ACTIVITIES

Republicans vs. Democrats

Divide the class into two groups to research either the Republican or the Democratic party. Several students in each group should work together to research and report on one of the following topics: origin, basic philosophy, notable leaders, or social, economic, environmental, or defense policies. Reports can include charts, graphs, illustrations, etc. Encourage students to include visual arrangements of material as well as written reports. Then have the students in each group work together to organize a presentation for the class.

Military Service and the Presidency

During the Clinton campaign, some people objected to the fact that Clinton had never been in the military and had avoided service in the Vietnam War. Have students form teams to find out which presidents served in the military and which did not. Post the results on the bulletin board.

Clinton Cartoons

Have each student select and bring to class three political cartoons on the subject of Clinton. Tell students to be prepared to explain the meaning of their cartoons during a class discussion. Post the best cartoons on a bulletin board. If the class sees a recurring theme (such as wavering on issues) in most of the cartoons, print it above them.

Bibliography

George Washington

Foster, Genevieve. *George Washington's World*. New York: Charles Scribner's Sons, 1941.

North, Sterling. *George Washington: Frontier Colonel*. New York: Random House, 1957.

John Adams

Bowen, Catherine Drinker. *John Adams and the American Revolution*. Boston: Little, Brown, 1950.

Peabody, James Bishop, ed. *John Adams: A Biography in His Own Words*. Newsweek Book Division, 1973, Vol. 1.

Thomas Jefferson

Moscow, Henry. *Thomas Jefferson and His World*. New York: Harper & Row, 1960, pp. 10–17.

Wibberly, Leonard. *The Gales of Spring: Thomas Jefferson, The Years 1789–1801*. New York: Farrar, Straus & Giroux, 1965.

James Madison

Fritz, Jean. *The Great Little Madison*. New York: G.P. Putnam, 1989, pp. 1–4.

Peterson, Merrill D., ed. *James Madison: A Biography in His Own Words*. New York: Harper & Row, 1974, pp. 14–18.

Rutland, Robert A. *James Madison, The Founding Father*. New York: Macmillan, 1987, pp. 8–10.

James Monroe

Cresson, William Penn. *James Monroe*. Chapel Hill, NC: University of North Carolina Press, 1946.

Hoyt, Edwin P. *James Monroe*. Reilly & Lee, 1968, pp. 3–8.

John Quincy Adams

Clarke, Fred G. *John Quincy Adams*. New York: Crowell-Collier, 1966.

Levin, Phyllis Lee. *Abigail Adams, A Biography*. New York: St. Martins Press, 1987, pp. 8–9.

Andrew Jackson

James, Marquis. *Andrew Jackson, The Border Captain*. New York: Grossett & Dunlap, 1959.

Ward, John William. *Andrew Jackson, Symbol for an Age*. Los Angeles: B. Jackson, 1955, pp. 1–20.

Martin Van Buren

Hoyt, Edwin P. *Martin Van Buren*. Reilly & Lee, 1964.

Wilson, Major L. *The Presidency of Martin Van Buren*. Lawrence, KS: University Press of Kansas, 1984, pp. 22–30.

William Henry Harrison

Fitz-Gerald, Christine Maloney. *William Henry Harrison*. Chicago: Children's Press, 1987, pp. 1–7.

Peterson, Norma Lois. *The Presidencies of William Henry Harrison and John Tyler*. Lawrence, KS: University Press of Kansas, 1989.

Sievers, Harry Joseph. *Benjamin Harrison: Hoosier Warrior*. Chicago: Henry Regnery Co., 1952, pp. 14–15.

John Tyler

Morgan, Robert J. *A Whig Embattled*. Lincoln, NE: University of Nebraska Press, 1954, pp. 53–56, 148–150.

Peterson, Norma Lois. *The Presidencies of William Henry Harrison and John Tyler*. Lawrence, KS: University Press of Kansas, 1989.

Seager, Robert II. *And Tyler Too: A Biography of John and Julia Tyler*. New York: McGraw-Hill, 1963.

James K. Polk

Gerson, Noel B. *The Slender Reed*. New York: Doubleday, 1965.

Lillegard, Dee. *James K. Polk*. Chicago: Children's Press, 1988, pp. 17–20.

Zachary Taylor

Bauer, K. Jack. *Zachary Taylor*. Baton Rouge, LA: Louisiana State University Press, 1985, pp. 6–12.

Kent, Zachary. *Zachary Taylor*. Chicago: Children's Press, 1988, pp. 15–18.

Millard Fillmore

Rayback, Robert J. *Millard Fillmore*. Newtown, CT: American Political Biography, 1972, pp. 2–6.

Franklin Pierce

Hoyt, Edwin P. *Franklin Pierce*. New York: Abelard-Schuman, 1972, pp. 18–23.

Nichols, Roy F. *Franklin Pierce: Young Hickory of the Granite Hills*. Philadelphia: University of Pennsylvania Press, 1931.

James Buchanan

Bell, Marlene Targ. *James Buchanan*. Chicago: Children's Press, 1988, pp. 13–23.

Hoyt, Edwin P. *James Buchanan*. Reilly & Lee, 1966.

Abraham Lincoln

Latham, Frank B. *Abraham Lincoln*. New York: Franklin Watts, 1968.

Thomas, Benjamin P. *Abraham Lincoln*. New York: Alfred A. Knopf, 1952, pp. 42–43.

Andrew Johnson

Dubowski, Cathy East. *Andrew Johnson*. Morristown, NJ: Silver Burdett Press, 1991, pp. 18–25.

Hoyt, Edwin P. *Andrew Johnson*. Reilly & Lee, 1965.

Ulysses S. Grant

Catton, Bruce. *Grant Moves South*. Boston: Little, Brown, 1960.

McFeely, William S. *Grant, A Biography*. New York: W.W. Norton, 1982, pp. 6–13.

Rutherford B. Hayes

Barnard, Harry. *Rutherford Hayes and His America*. Newtown, CT: American Political Biography, 1954.

Williams, Harry. *Hayes of the Twenty-Third*. New York: Alfred A. Knopf, 1965.

James A. Garfield

Hoyt, Edwin P. *James A. Garfield*. Reilly & Lee, 1964.

Taylor, John M. *Garfield of Ohio: The Available Man*. New York: W.W. Norton, 1970, pp. 30–36.

Chester A. Arthur

Howe, George F. *Chester A. Arthur: A Quarter Century of Machine Politics*. New York: Frederick Ungar, 1934.

Reeves, Thomas C. *Gentleman Boss: The Life of Chester Alan Arthur*. New York: Alfred A. Knopf, 1975, pp. 3–14.

Grover Cleveland

Hoyt, Edwin P. *Grover Cleveland*. Reilly & Lee, 1962.

Tugwell, Guy Rexford. *Grover Cleveland*. New York: Macmillan, 1968.

Benjamin Harrison

Sievers, Harry Joseph. *Benjamin Harrison: Hoosier Warrior*. Chicago: Henry Regnery Co., 1952, pp. 20–30.

William McKinley

Kent, Zachary. *William McKinley*. Chicago: Children's Press, 1988.

Leech, Margaret K. *In the Days of McKinley*. New York: Harper & Row, 1959.

Morgan, H.W. *William McKinley and His America*. Syracuse, NY: Syracuse University Press, 1963.

Theodore Roosevelt

Cooper, John Milton, Jr. *The Warrior and the Priest: Woodrow Wilson and Theodore Roosevelt*. Cambridge, MA: Belknap Press, 1983, pp. 5–10.

Hagedorn, Hermann. *The Roosevelt Family of Sagamore Hill*. New York: Macmillan, 1954, p. 6.

Morris, Edmund. *The Rise of Theodore Roosevelt*. New York: Coward McCann Geoghegan, 1979, pp. 37–55.

William Howard Taft

Duffy, Herb S. *William Howard Taft*. Balch & Co., 1930, p. 5.

Pringle, Henry. *William Howard Taft*. New York: Farrar & Rinehart, 1939.

Ross, Ishbel. *The Tafts, An American Family 1678–1964*. Cleveland, OH: World Publishing Company, 1964.

Woodrow Wilson

Cooper, John Milton, Jr. *The Warrior and the Priest: Woodrow Wilson and Theodore Roosevelt.* Cambridge, MA: Belknap Press, 1983, pp. 6–21.

Hatch, Alden. Woodrow Wilson: A Biography. New York: Holt, Rinehart and Winston, 1947.

Warren G. Harding

Adams, Samuel Hopkins. *Incredible Era: The Life and Times of Warren Gamaliel Harding.* New York: G.P. Putnam, 1964, pp. 1–14.

Sinclair, Andrew. *The Available Man: The Life Behind the Masks of Warren Gamaliel Harding.* New York: Macmillan, 1965, pp. 7–14.

Calvin Coolidge

McCoy, Donald R. *Calvin Coolidge.* New York: Macmillan, 1967, pp. 1–10.

White, William A. *A Puritan in Babylon, the Story of Calvin Coolidge.* New York: G.P. Putnam, 1965.

Herbert Hoover

Burner, David. *Herbert Hoover, a Public Life.* New York: Alfred A. Knopf, 1979, pp. 7–15.

Hoover, Herbert. *The Memoirs of Herbert Hoover,* Vol I. New York: Macmillan, 1952.

McGee, Dorothy H. *Herbert Hoover: Engineer, Humanitarian, Statesman.* New York: Dodd & Mead, 1965.

Franklin Delano Roosevelt

Freidel, Frank. *Franklin Delano Roosevelt,* Vol I. Boston: Little, Brown, 1952.

Israel, Fred L. *Franklin Delano Roosevelt.* New York: Chelsea House, 1985, pp. 15–18.

Johnson, Gerald W. *Franklin D. Roosevelt.* New York: William Morrow & Co., 1967, pp. 18–35.

Osinski, Alice. *Franklin Roosevelt.* Chicago: Children's Press, 1987, pp. 11–26.

Harry S Truman

Hillman, William. *Mr. President.* New York: Farrar, Straus & Young, 1952.

Martin, Ralph G. *President From Missouri: Harry S Truman.* New York: Julian Messner, 1964, pp. 9–25.

Truman, Harry S. *Memoirs,* Vol. 1. New York: Doubleday, 1955.

Dwight D. Eisenhower

Neal, Steve. *The Eisenhowers, Reluctant Dynasty.* New York: Doubleday, 1978, pp. 1–20.

Pusey, M.J. *Eisenhower, the President.* New York: Macmillan, 1956.

Sandberg, Peter Lars. *Dwight D. Eisenhower.* New York: Chelsea House, 1986, pp. 19–23.

John F. Kennedy

Faber, Harold, ed. *The Kennedy Years.* New York: Viking Press, 1964, pp. 16–19.

Kennedy, Rose Fitzgerald. *Times to Remember.* New York: Doubleday, 1974, pp. 93–183.

McTaggart, Lynn. *Kathleen Kennedy, Her Life and Times.* New York: Doubleday, 1983, pp. 9–10.

Lyndon B. Johnson

Kearns, Doris. *Lyndon Johnson and the American Dream.* New York: Harper & Row, 1976, pp. 26–36.

Mooney, Booth. *The Lyndon Johnson Story.* New York: Farrar, Straus & Giroux, 1964.

Richard M. Nixon

Ambrose, Stephen. *Nixon: The Education of a Politician,* Vol. 1. New York: Simon & Schuster, 1987, pp. 1–39.

Nadel, Laurie. *The Great Stream of History: A Biography of Richard Nixon.* New York: Atheneum, 1991, pp. 3–17.

Gerald Ford

Ford, Gerald. *A Time to Heal, an Autobiography.* Harper & Row, 1979.

Reeves, Richard. *Gerald Ford: A Ford, not a Lincoln.* Harcourt Brace Jovanovich, 1975.

Jimmy Carter

Carter, Jimmy. *Keeping Faith: Memoirs of a President.* Bantam, 1982.

Smith, Betsy Covington. *Jimmy Carter, President.* New York: Walker & Co., 1986, pp. 12–20.

Ronald Reagan

Edwards, Anne. *Early Reagan*. William Morrow & Co., 1987, pp. 14–64.

Reagan, Ronald. *An American Life*. Simon & Schuster, 1990.

George Bush

Bush, George. *Looking Forward*. Doubleday, 1987.

Hyams, Joe. *Flight of the Avenger*. Harcourt Brace Jovanovich, 1991, pp. 16–26.

Bill Clinton

Allen, Charles F. and Portis, Jonathan. *The Comeback Kid: The Life and Career of Bill Clinton*. New York: Birch Lane Press, 1992, pp. 3–10.

Isaacson, Walter. "A Time for Courage," *Time* magazine, November 3, 1992, pp. 26–29.

Kramer, Michael. "What He Will Do," *Time* magazine, November 3, 1992, pp. 31–32.